SKATING DRILLS
— FOR —
HOCKEY

SKATING DRILLS
FOR
HOCKEY

Dr. Randy Gregg

OVER TIME BOOKS

The Publisher: OverTime Books is an imprint of Éditions de la Montagne Verte

Library and Archives Canada Cataloguing in Publication

Gregg, Randy, 1956–
    Skating drills for hockey / Randy Gregg.

    ISBN-13: 978-0-9737681-5-2
    ISBN-10: 0-9737681-5-0

    1. Hockey—Training. I. Title. II. Series

GV848.3G742006   796.962'2   C06-911192-1

Project Director: J. Alexander Poulton
Illustrator: Ross Palsson
Cover Image: Dave Vasicek, Colorspace Photo-Graphics

PC:P5

Dedication

To my son Jamie,
who shows me every time he participates in sport
how important commitment, hard work
and mental focus is to the success of an athlete
and a team

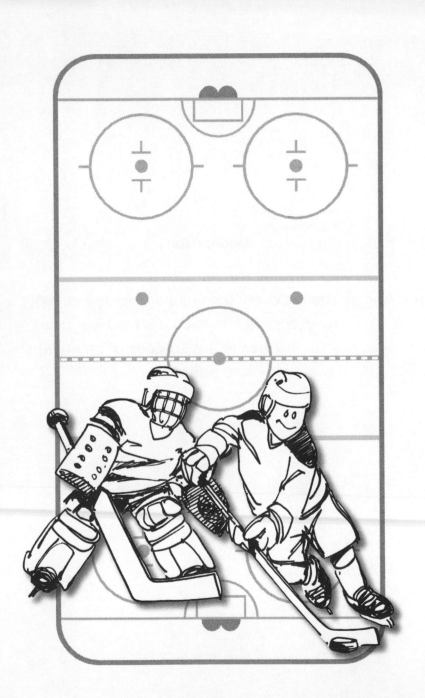

Contents

Introduction

MY HOCKEY EXPERIENCE BEGAN LIKE THOUSANDS OF OTHERS, in the backyard of my parents' house. My father was an engineer for the railroad and on his days off he would flood a small area of grass outside our back door. As the youngest of six children, I had several siblings who acted as enthusiastic coaches, trying to teach me the proper technique of skating on our five-meter (15-foot) square hockey rink. Like most adult skaters, I remember it like it was yesterday, pushing a folding chair around the ice, trying not to land on my rear end, while attempting to impress my brothers and sisters like I was a "pro" skating through center ice at Maple Leaf Gardens.

As I got older, my size and interest in hockey outgrew our backyard rink, and my friends and I progressed to the local community rink. It was located directly across from the elementary school that I attended—Inglewood School. My mother made sure that supper was ready and finished by 5:30 PM because we were out the door with skates and stick in hand anticipating another full night of hockey fun. The recreational skaters took over the main rink at 6 PM; sticks weren't allowed on that ice surface so all the hockey players converged on the half-sized rink out back. We spent hours and hours playing games, practicing shots, and generally hanging out in that pint-sized rink. Occasionally, when we got tired, some of us would go to the big rink and start a game of tag or keep away, much to the dismay of the girls who were pleasantly skating around and around the ice to the sounds of winter music.

My first opportunity to play an actual game of hockey came at age five, in the house league community schedule. I was chosen to play on the "Chicago Blackhawks" along with my best friend, who was a goaltender. What a thrill it was to don that jersey for the first time, not only because I was finally a member of a hockey team, but because the great Blackhawk, Bobby Hull, was my idol. We won our first game easily. My friend got a shutout, and I scored 11 goals. I'd like to think that it was because of my superb talent; however, my success in scoring was simply because I knew how to skate and the others didn't! That scoring prowess didn't last through my minor hockey years. Actually, that may have been a good thing since I'm sure I would have ended up with a swollen head!

From ages seven to nineteen, my hockey experience was fulfilling, each year playing with friends on teams both in my community and on zone teams. I was fortunate to have coaches who believed that the game should be competitive, but more importantly, that every player should have a great time. None of the coaches were highly skilled from a technical standpoint but that didn't matter to us. We weren't good enough players to know the difference, but we did realize that our coaches were fair and honest, and treated everyone equally. At the end of every season, we left the rink hardly able to wait for the next season to begin, a testimony to the success of our amateur coaches.

My hockey career took a quantum leap in 1975, my first year of medical school. My older brother Ron told me in no uncertain terms that I would have to quit playing baseball, hockey and all my other sports in order to devote all my time to my medical studies. Early in September, the University of Alberta Golden Bears hockey team staged tryouts for anyone who wanted to come. A few of my friends were going, so I thought that I would go out for a couple of free skates before being released and refocusing on my medical studies. Fortunately for me, Golden Bears coach

Leon Abbott saw something in this tall lanky defenseman and decided to give me a shot with the team. Hesitant at first, I decided that I would play for the Bears as long as it didn't interfere with my studies. Four years and two national championships later, some of my fondest memories in sport had concluded. Because of the exposure to college coaches like Abbott, Clare Drake and Billy Moores, I had transformed from a slow, lanky minor hockey player to a not-quite-so-slow, lanky defenseman who knew how to play the game. With the help of great instructors and role models at university, I learned a great deal about medicine and just as much about the techniques, strategies and discipline required to be a good hockey player.

Playing college hockey and going to medical school wasn't the easiest thing I had ever done. Often I would have to slip out the back door of the lecture theater 15 minutes before the end of classes in order to get to practice on time. Dryland training was impossible for me most weeks. Just getting to all the practices and games was a big enough chore. That all changed when I graduated from medical school and was fortunate to join Canada's 1980 Olympic hockey team. It was there that for the first time in my life I was able to give a 100% commitment to becoming the best player I could be. Even as early as 1980, the Olympic program placed a great deal of emphasis on the three components of the game—the technical, the physical and the mental. Up until this point in my life, I had been exposed to dozens of coaches whose primary responsibility was to teach the technical aspects of the game, such as skating, passing, stickhandling and so on. My first Olympic experience expanded my hockey world into the areas of elite physical training and mental toughness. Coaches like

Clare Drake, Lorne Davis and Tom Watt were instrumental in designing a physical training program that would augment our daily on-ice training program. Father David Bauer, the mentor behind Canada's Olympic chances in Lake Placid, provided an unforgettable wealth of knowledge that focused on discipline, mental preparedness and perspectives in sport. Though it may be hard to believe, this combination of personal and physical development turned a sixth place finish in the 1980 Olympics into the greatest sporting experience of my life!

The opportunity to play professionally in the National Hockey League was not only a great challenge but also a perfect chance to experience a variety of coaching styles and practice philosophies. Some NHL coaches would often have their teams on the ice for hours at a time, while others were well prepared and never ran a practice over 60 minutes. It was fascinating to watch how the greatest players in the world responded to these different coaching styles and practice plans. I tried to analyze which of the practice plans and specifically which drills the players received most positively. I also noticed how the tempo of a practice plummeted when certain things happened—usually situations that the coach in charge was not aware of at all.

I am pleased to write this hockey drill book as a tribute to all the men and women who came before me and their efforts to make the game of hockey as enjoyable and exciting as possible for players of all ages. I hope coaches can use the drills and the information to enhance the quality of hockey experience that they are providing for their players.

Yours in sporting,

Randy

Skills-Based Learning

LIKE MOST TEAM SPORTS, HOCKEY IS AN INTEGRATED GAME. Players must learn the individual skills necessary to be a competent player. A young athlete must then learn how to use these skills in a team environment so that team performance is maximized. As a player progresses to a more competitive hockey environment, there is an increased emphasis on physical conditioning using on-ice and dryland training. However, in addition to skill mastery and the physical part of the game, it is mental strength that can often separate elite hockey players from true superstars.

Although the individual abilities of hockey players vary widely from youth to adolescence to adulthood, the skills they must possess to become better are similar. There are 10 skills that are of primary importance in the development of a hockey player. These include skating speed, agility, power, stickhandling, passing, shooting, checking, positional play, intuition and work ethic. It is important to emphasize the development of these skills at every practice.

In organized minor hockey, players are seldom coached by the same person for more than one season. Inevitably, each year players must adapt to yet another coaching style and temperament. This may not be such a bad thing because it gives the young players a wide range of experience so they can judge for themselves what type of coach or practice makes them perform at optimal levels. However, the main problem with exposing young players to a different coach every year is the variability in how each one teaches the 10 fundamental hockey skills.

An analogy with formal schooling is appropriate. Does a Grade Four math teacher develop and teach a system of learning to calculate fractions only to have the Grade Five teacher create a completely new system? Of course not. The school system was developed with an organized, consistent approach to learning so that students get the best chance to excel in all the subjects. Curricula are established and then closely followed by teachers from year to year so that every child has an equal opportunity to learn.

In hockey, well-meaning and enthusiastic volunteers give their time freely "to help the kids." Without volunteer coaching ranks, it would not be possible for the vast majority of youngsters to play hockey. Thirty years ago, Father David Bauer believed that it would be best if hockey was integrated into the school system to ensure consistent instruction for all players. Over the years there have been a number of excellent programs for coaches to become even better teachers on the ice. I hope that this manual can provide some valuable tools that will make this directed focus on teaching at practice even more successful.

SKILLS-BASED LEARNING

How to Use this Book

IN VIRTUALLY EVERY ASPECT OF SOCIETY, PREPARATION and planning are two vital steps toward success in any endeavor. Teachers prepare lesson plans for their daily classes, doctors prepare for surgical procedures and truck drivers plan their routes before embarking on a trip. Similarly, it is imperative that coaches plan and prepare for each practice. Having an overall objective for each practice is essential. The objective for a particular practice may be skating, breakouts, power play or defensive zone play, but it is important that the objectives for individual practices also further the overall goal of building a team that works well together. It is important to select practice drills that best suit the needs of the team at that particular stage of the season. This book describes many skating drills that can be used to develop a strong practice plan. Puck control, team, advanced and goalie drills can be found in Books 2–4.

Five Guidelines for Practice Planning

When developing a practice plan, follow these five main guidelines in order to maximize a team's practice potential:

1.	Be prepared—make a practice plan.
2.	Use progressive skill learning through drill expansion.
3.	Work on each individual skill during each practice.
4.	Use technical and dynamic drills in appropriate situations.
5.	Make practices fun.

Be prepared—make a practice plan

Coaches expect every player to come to practice with skates, stick and other equipment in hand, ready to work hard for the entire one-hour practice. Similarly, players and parents should expect the coaching staff to be ready to run an effective, well-organized practice with drills that challenge and stimulate players in every position. As in many other teaching professions, a written plan is a valuable tool for two reasons:

1. Making a practice plan requires that a coach spend time the night before thinking about the strengths and weaknesses of his team and how it can improve. Then the coach can choose specific drills, to focus on learning in those areas of weakness. A written practice plan is easy to follow and provides a focus for the practice, ensuring that ice time is used most efficiently.

2. Watching a coach who regularly checks his written plan gives parents in the stands confidence that the practice has been well thought through and will be worthwhile for their children. Demonstrating a high level of preparation is an important step to gaining parents' confidence towards the decisions made during each game of the season.

Use progressive skill learning
through drill expansion

Shortly after retiring from the National Hockey League, I had the opportunity to coach my young sons in organized youth hockey. Although it was quite obvious that their skill level was low, I tried the same drills that I had used in NHL practices. Of course, I had to scale back both the complexity and intensity of the drills to fit the level of my little team. I was pleased to see that, not only did these young seven- and eight-year-olds pick up the idea behind the drills quickly, but practices were high paced, fun and a wealth of learning for the players. I realized then that the skills of hockey are no different whether at the atom or the professional level. It was simply a matter of establishing the level of complexity that could be handled by the players in question. The concept of drill expansion was born. It excited me to think that young hockey players could go through their entire minor hockey experience practicing a set of drills that were consistent yet constantly expanding in intensity and complexity. Novice players, Bantam players and Olympians can use a similar set of drills that provide a consistent approach to teaching the skills of the game. This idea is, of course, no different than what the school system did years ago when they developed standardized teaching curricula in the core school subjects so that all students benefit from formal education. That has always sounded like a worthy goal for hockey organizations. However, because the system relies on volunteer coaches who have diverse backgrounds and who often change from year to year, the idea of a common coaching strategy with regards to practice organization is still in its infancy.

The Canadian Hockey Association and USA Hockey have done a remarkable job in developing coaching seminars and clinics to provide coaches with a stronger background in hockey knowledge. This book is intended to be a useful, practical tool for coaches interested in offering the best practices available to their players. Sample practice plans and practice templates have been included in the book to make it easy for a coach at any hockey level to expand his skills in practice planning and organization. Refer to *Puck Control Drills for Hockey* (Book 2), *Team Drills for Hockey* (Book 3) and *Advanced Drills & Goalie Drills for Hockey* (Book 4) for other drills to complete your practice.

Work on each individual skill during each practice

Having a major theme or objective in mind is a good idea when planning a hockey practice. If the team is struggling with passing or defensive positioning, then it would be productive to include specific drills that focus on those areas. It is also important to consider including at least one drill to work each of the specific individual hockey skills while progressing through practice. Following a good warmup, it is important to work on skating, stickhandling, passing, shooting and checking skills in every practice before requiring players to perform the more dynamic team-oriented drills. It has been said a solid house is built on a strong foundation, and there is no doubt that the foundation of a good hockey player is the mastery of individual technical skills!

Use technical and dynamic drills effectively

Because teaching the various aspects of the game of hockey can be complicated in both its individual and team responsibilities, it is important that coaches help players develop new skills in a slow and progressive way. Attempting to teach a sophisticated defensive breakout system to a group of first-year players is a recipe for disaster. Fortunately, most hockey skills can be taught in two ways— technically and dynamically.

In this manual you will notice that the drills are divided into two basic groupings:

- **Technical drills** are designed to decrease the complexity of the rink environment so that players can focus totally on one specific skill. This is a time when coaches can easily approach individual players to work on teaching changes to their technique in a particular area. A good example of a technical drill would be the Stationary Pass Drill, where players stand in one location working with a partner on receiving and making good passes.

- **Dynamic drills** are designed to integrate the exciting aspects of hockey, including speed, finesse, positional play and checking. These drills are effective in developing the same individual technical skills but are set in an environment that more closely resembles a regular game setting. Because these drills are run at a faster pace, several external stimuli are present that challenge each player to be even more aware of the entire game setting. Do not try dynamic drills until all players have almost mastered the technical drills that teach similar hockey skills in isolation. For more experienced players, this kind of drill most closely simulates game situations where many things are happening on the ice at one time.

Drill Favorites Icon: Several drills in the book are identified with this icon. These are my favorite drills in each of the skill sections. They are drills that are applicable at any age level in hockey, and I strongly recommend them to any coach. Even the best hockey coach does not need thousands of drills in order to improve his team. He simply needs a core of 10 or 20 drills that he feels comfortable with to properly develop his players' individual and team skills.

 Level of Difficulty Icon: All of the drills in this book have been assigned a level of difficulty, which provides a sense of how and when a particular drill should be included in planning a practice. A drill with Level 1 difficulty can be easily carried out by beginning players, while a drill with Level 4 difficulty is quite complex and should be reserved for more experienced, competitive players.

It is necessary to first evaluate the level of talent on the team. From that assessment, determine the level of difficulty that is most appropriate for the drills to include in a practice plan.

Make practices fun

There continues to be a small group of coaches, managers
and parents who believe that players cannot develop the
ultimate commitment to hockey if they have fun during practice. A smiling, joking player who enjoys the social aspect of
hockey to the same degree as he enjoys the physical aspect
has in the past been looked upon as being soft or lacking
discipline. Luckily, this attitude is quickly going the way of
the dinosaur!

For the vast majority of amateur hockey players, the number one reason why they play hockey is to have fun with
their friends. Although many dream of a professional career,
the reality for most is that success will likely be measured
by simply continuing through the minor hockey ranks and
enjoying the game so much that they continue to play into
adulthood. Hockey is a fine game with its speed, finesse,
tactics and emphasis on teamwork. Every child who is
interested should have the opportunity to participate in the
game at a level that is best suited for him skillwise, socially,
and financially.

Coaches who berate players, punish them with excessive skating or who verbally criticize young referees in front of their teams have little grasp of the great influence they really have on their players. Hockey continues to struggle to keep its players from turning to sports that offer recreation at a lower cost. Many hockey experts believe that a major turnaround in attitude towards the teaching of hockey is needed in order to return hockey to its position of glory in the cultural makeup of our country.

So what can a coach do to ensure that each player on his team enjoys the sport of hockey to its utmost? From a psychological standpoint, there are many ways a coach can help build self-esteem, create a non-threatening dressing room environment and assist in developing long-term friendships among the team members. Unfortunately, this topic is outside the scope of this book. For further details and a more comprehensive reference on coaching philosophy, injury identification, proper nutrition and skill enhancement, please refer to *Hockey: The Technical, the Physical, and the Mental Game.**

Every morning on a game day, National Hockey League teams have a pre-game skate. It is usually just a quick workout so that players can stretch out and work on some flow drills before the evening game. During my time with the Edmonton Oilers, the real practice often began once the coaches left the ice. Players would surround the center ice circle and begin a rousing game of Pig in the Middle. We would play that game for what seemed like hours, working on our passing and receiving, but mostly just having a great time. The memories of players like Gretzky and Messier laughing and joking during the simple game that I now use with my young teams will stay with me forever. Many people wonder why some players become truly great superstars. Part of the puzzle is undoubtedly physical talent, but I am sure that a big part of hockey success also comes from this intense love of playing the game.

---

* *Hockey: The Technical, the Physical, and the Mental Game* by Dr. Randy Gregg.
©1999, FP Hendriks Publishing Ltd.

During practices coaches can do several things to ensure that players enjoy their hockey experience:

1. **Have a positive attitude.**
   Every hockey player makes mistakes. If we focus on what people can do rather than what they can't, then we develop willing and eager players.

2. **Maintain a high tempo at practice.**
   One easy way that players lose interest in the game is when they must endure a poorly organized and boring practice. Make it fast and make it fun!

3. **Lead by example; be energetic.**
   It's hard for a player to give all he has if his coach and role model is lethargic, bored and appears to be disinterested.

4. **Be fair.**
   The quickest way to lose your players' respect is to show favoritism to your own child or to the players on the team who are more skilled.

5. **Run practices efficiently.**
   The main reason coaches must extend practices past one hour for minor hockey players is because they are not well prepared. Short, high-tempo practices make for good skill challenges and happy players!

6. **Include at least one fun drill at the end of practice.**
   Would you rather have your players spend the three or four days before next practice remembering how sick they felt after a hard punishing skate, or would you rather they remember the excitement and fun of playing a challenging game that also helped to improve their hockey skills? The answer seems obvious to most. Please refer to Book 4 *(Advanced Drills & Goalie Drills for Hockey)* for some effective ideas that can be used during each practice.

A Note about Male and Female Hockey

You will notice throughout this book that I use the words *he*, *him*, and *his* when describing hockey players and coaches. I do this only for ease of reading, not because of a bias towards male dominance in hockey. It is exciting to see the number of female hockey teams sprouting up in amateur hockey leagues across the country, as well as the development of many very capable and experienced female coaches. Hockey is the type of dynamic, fast-paced game that should be enjoyed by all youngsters, big or small, rich or poor, skilled or inexperienced, male or female. It is encouraging to see interest in female hockey increase, from novice levels all the way up to participation in the Olympic Games!

Even the best hockey coach does not need thousands of drills in order to improve his team. He simply needs a core of 10 or 20 drills that he feels comfortable with to properly develop his players' individual and team skills.

Skating Drills

Skating

Definition—*the ability to propel oneself across the ice while wearing skates*

IT IS ALMOST IMPOSSIBLE TO PLAY SOCCER IF YOU CANNOT run. Likewise, it is difficult to play volleyball if you cannot jump. In hockey, a player can be an accomplished stickhandler or shooter, but unless he can skate well, the game will always continue to be a struggle.

Skating Drill Organization

Although specific areas of skating are addressed in further chapters, comments and drills that work on general skating skills are important to consider. I have strayed from the grouping of technical and dynamic drills in this chapter, because I believe there is a better way to consider the organization of general skating drills. I have broken the following skating drills into linear, directional and conditioning.

1. **Linear Skating.** These drills emphasize the importance of learning how to propel oneself as effectively as possible in a straight, forward line. This is important in game situations where players are back-checking or racing for a loose puck in anticipation of a breakaway.

2. **Directional Skating.** These drills emphasize the importance of quick directional changes and are effective in developing a player's agility, coordination and balance.

3. Conditioning Skating. There are many opinions in hockey with regards to conditioning skating during regular on-ice practices. Each year parents send their children to conditioning camps prior to the upcoming hockey season. There are many coaches who use conditioning drills at the end of practice to keep their players in good shape. Still other coaches use conditioning skating drills to punish the team for playing poorly in the previous game.

To understand what may be the best approach for our own children and their teams, it is necessary to closely examine just what conditioning for hockey really means. It is well known that a good aerobic fitness base is important to maintain the intensity of play during a 60-minute hockey game. Aerobic conditioning is typically regarded as submaximal intensity activity that lasts for at least 20 or 30 minutes. A runner, for instance, will usually average a minimum of a 30-minute run two or three times a week to maintain a good level of aerobic fitness. That runner would try to maintain a heart rate at about 70 percent of its maximum to achieve optimal benefits.

The formula above gives only a general idea of the degree of intensity to work at during exercise. A 20-year-old hockey player would work at a proper exercise intensity if his heart rate was $(220 - 20) \times 70\% = 140$ beats per minute.

To achieve an optimum degree of aerobic training in a hockey environment, coaches would have to spend almost half their practice on conditioning skating drills. Imagine the lost potential for skill development in the areas of stickhandling, shooting, passing, checking and other valuable technical components of the game.

SKATING

Here is a simple formula to estimate what a person's maximum heart rate during exercise should be:

Maximum Heart Rate = 220 – Person's Age

A simple solution to on-ice conditioning is to keep the tempo of the practices high, with few breaks for on-ice discussion. In this way, each player is subjected to a full hour of conditioning training while they are working on their technical hockey skills. There is no need to spend the last 15 minutes of every practice doing skating drills, unless of course, they incorporate a component of a technical skating skill such as speed, agility or power.

Early in my hockey career, I learned to consider this formula as only a very general estimate. Prior to the 1980 Winter Olympic Games, our players were subjected to maximum heart rate testing where we had to ride a stationary bike until exhaustion. It was interesting to see that as hard as I tried, I could only get my heart rate up to 165 beats per minute. A teammate of mine with similar build and age had a maximum heart rate of 215! So much for standard calculations.

In the future, the emergence of dryland training for hockey players of all ages will replace the need for on-ice conditioning as we know it. Players and coaches will have the insight and knowledge to plan and carry out less expensive, creative and fun conditioning activities in gyms, parks or community halls, both during the season and throughout the off-season. Stationary bike intervals, Aeroball, Ultimate Football and in-line skating programs are only a few examples of enjoyable activities that players of all ages can easily participate in.

For those coaches who still believe that a small part of every practice should include conditioning skating, I have included a couple of my favorites. I especially like these drills because they incorporate high-speed skating along with their conditioning components. As we continue to see in the National Hockey League, the focus on elite player selection continues to sway towards those who have blistering speed, as all the other technical hockey skills can be improved with repetitive practice. Keep this in mind: "Low intensity, slow practice drills make low intensity, slow players."

Low intensity, slow practice drills make low intensity, slow players.

SKATING

Linear Skating

LINEAR SKATING, SIMPLY PUT, IS SKATING FORWARD IN
a straight line. For effective linear skating, coaches should
encourage players to keep their knees well bent so that they
can fully push to the side during their stride. Unfortunately,
many young players have not yet developed strong muscles in
their legs and find it difficult to skate with bent knees. As they
get older and participate in drills that strengthen the thigh
muscles, players will become more effective skaters. It is also
important to encourage players to keep their heads up while
skating so that they can see the play around them and quickly
assess and anticipate a potential change in direction. In addition, arm movement is an effective way to get additional
momentum in a forward direction, yet few young skaters learn
the proper way to move their arms while skating. Swinging
arms from side to side while skating tends to be counter-
productive, as no additional
momentum in a forward
direction is created.

Finally, it is necessary to encourage players to keep their sticks close to the ice while skating so that they get used to a stick position that is ready to receive a pass at any time. Along with keeping sticks on the ice, teach players to extend their sticks forward and back during the skating stride so that arm movement provides momentum in a forward direction. This is a difficult skill, especially for young players, but it is crucial in terms of allowing a player to develop his ultimate skating potential.

Goalies should be expected to perform skating drills along with the team.

On the following pages are drills that focus on linear skating skills. Mastery of linear skating is the foundation for more game-oriented directional skating. Goalies should be expected to perform skating drills along with the team.

LINEAR SKATING

Skating Fundamentals

Objective
To develop proper leg extension to the side

Description
- Line players up at one end of the rink, half on the end zone line and the other half immediately behind them.
- The players assume the basic skating position with their elbows close to touching their knees.
- On a whistle, the first group begins skating while thrusting only one leg outward, striding down the ice.
- Once the first group reaches the near blue line, the second group begins.
- Have players switch to the other leg when coming back down the ice.

Key Teaching Points
- Start in basic skating position with knees bent close to ninety degrees.
- Encourage players to direct leg pushes out to the side, not backwards.
- During leg push, ensure players fully extend the knee to get maximum efficiency with every stride.
- Encourage players to keep their torsos down—no bobbing up and down.
- Emphasize bent knees and full leg thrust, not speed or racing.

EXPANSION

#1. Players fully extend both legs while moving down the ice, making sure to stay in proper skating position.

#2. Players try a lateral jump push—jump from side to side while striding, maintaining balance on the landing leg at all times, and developing explosive leg extension.

Angle Board Skating

Objective
To develop stopping and quick direction-changing skills

Description
- Players start in one corner of the rink.
- The first player moves with quick speed towards the near blue line across the other side of the rink.
- Once the first player reaches the middle of the rink, the next player begins the drill.
- They execute two-footed stops and pivot, skating hard to the opposite centerline.
- Players continue to the other blue line and the far corner.

Key Teaching Points
- Encourage quick acceleration on the first three strides.
- Encourage players to execute two-footed stops and accelerate quickly in the opposite direction.
- Encourage players to practice stopping on both skate edges.
- Ensure that the first few strides are explosive, working on speed training.
- Ensure players keep their knees bent when changing directions.

EXPANSION

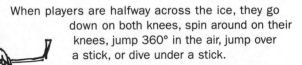

When players are halfway across the ice, they go down on both knees, spin around on their knees, jump 360° in the air, jump over a stick, or dive under a stick.

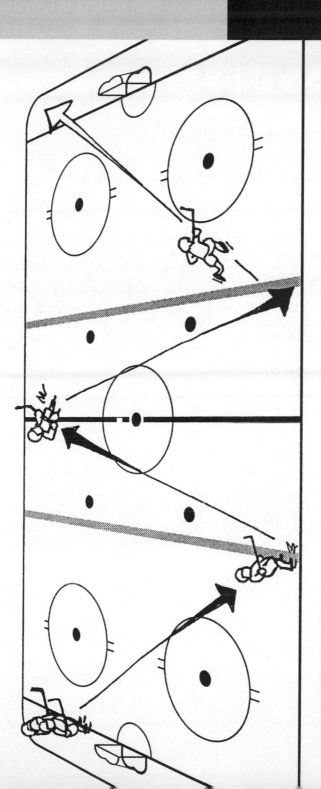

ANGLE BOARD
SKATING

Long-Stride Skating

Objective
To develop full leg extension while skating

Description
- Players skate down one side of the rink using regular warmup skating.
- They then skate down the other side of the rink using exaggerated long strides.
- Observe the players as they skate to ensure that every player fully extends his push-off leg with each stride.

Key Teaching Points
- Encourage players to extend legs to the maximum with each push off.
- Encourage players to keep their knees bent when the knee is directly under the body.
- Emphasize full extension of the legs at a low rate of skating speed.
- Speed is not of utmost importance; full leg extension is!

1
2
3
4

Inside Outside Edge

Objective
To develop stopping and quick direction-changing skills

Description
- Players start in one corner of the rink.
- The first player moves with quick speed towards the near blue line across the other side of the rink.
- Once the first player reaches the middle of the rink, the next player begins the drill.
- They execute two-footed stops and pivot, skating hard to the opposite centerline.
- Players continue to the other blue line and the far corner.

Key Teaching Points
- Encourage quick acceleration on the first three strides.
- Encourage players to execute two-footed stops and accelerate quickly in the opposite direction.
- Encourage players to practice stopping on both skate edges.
- Ensure that the first few strides are explosive, working on speed and training.
- Ensure players keep knees bent when changing directions.
- Ensure players keep knees bent with a low center of gravity.
- Have players work to lengthen their lateral strides.

1
2
3
4

Crossover using outside edge

Leg thrust using inside edge and wide-stance skating

INSIDE OUTSIDE EDGE

Forward-Backward-Forward Skating

Objective

To develop proper pivoting technique with acceleration

Description

- Players perform full-ice circle skating in one direction.
- They skate forward around the nets then turn at the blue line and skate backward.
- Players change to forward skating at the far blue line.
- They work on hop jump from forward to backward.
- Players try both crossover and pivot turns from backward to forward skating.
- They work on both C-cut (the backward stride that doesn't require any leg crossovers) and crossover backward skating.
- Players perform strong forward crossover skating around the nets.

Key Teaching Points

- Encourage players to always turn facing the boards.
- Encourage players to keep knees bent for best agility.
- Encourage use of the first few strides to accelerate quickly after pivoting.
- Players perform the drill in both directions around the ice.

Directional Skating

WITH BOTH LINEAR SKATING AND DIRECTIONAL SKATING, it is vital that young players be taught to skate with bent knees. Not only does it allow players to get a stronger push-off during every skating stride, but it also ensures that they have a lower center of gravity and allows them to change direction more effectively while skating. The ability to master the use of both inside and outside skate edges is often difficult for young players to learn.

Imagine a hockey player who has blinding one-directional speed and can turn on a dime, accelerating quickly in the opposite direction. Every coach would love to have players like this. To this end, use practice drills that challenge players to develop a strong push-off with both legs, as well as the ability to cross over and turn in both directions with equal efficiency. Although there are excellent drills that can be used to specifically improve directional skating, this skill is practiced in almost all dynamic, game situation drills.

On the following pages are drills that focus on directional skating skills in order to produce an entire team of players who can skate efficiently and change direction quickly and effectively. An experienced coach will challenge players to improve their directional skating in two ways:

1. He will incorporate technical drills into a practice where the coaching staff can evaluate and give feedback on each player's skating skills.

2. He will run practices at a high tempo so that during the dynamic stickhandling, passing, shooting, checking and team drills, the players continue to improve their directional skating skills.

Goalies should be expected to perform skating drills along with the team.

DIRECTIONAL SKATING

Double-Circle Warmup

Objective
To develop a consistent, dynamic on-ice stretching drill

Description
- This can be the first drill in all of your practices, beginning once all players are on the ice and following an introductory talk about the practice.
- Players skate half speed through the middle of the ice and as they reach the end zone, curl into either corner, skating back down the boards in the opposite direction. The drill is continuous in a double-circle skating direction.
- A coach stands stationary in the center of the blue line where the players begin skating through the middle of the ice, demonstrating the stretch that he wants the players to try as they skate through the mid-ice area.
- Two other coaches are located at the far outside blue lines encouraging the players to practice long strides with full leg extension as they skate down the outside of the rink.
- The drill continues until each player has stretched the shoulders, arms, back and legs in this dynamic stretching drill.

Key Teaching Points
- Encourage players to keep skating while they stretch.
- Emphasize long, slower strides down the outside of the ice while stretching through the middle.
- The long-stride skating practice is designed to encourage full leg extension and should not be a race of any kind.

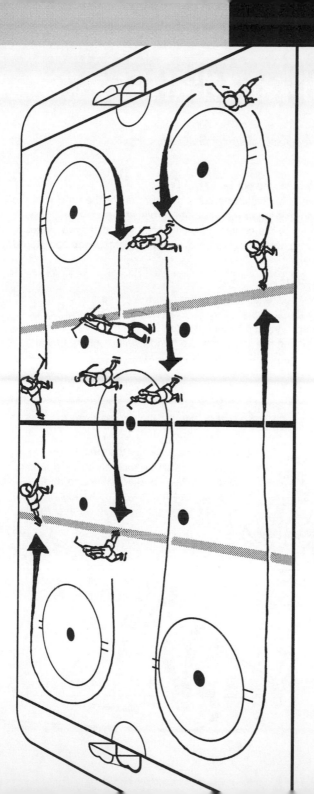

DOUBLE-CIRCLE WARMUP

Five-Circle Skating

Objective
To develop the proper technique for crossovers

Description
- Start all players in one corner of the rink.
- The first three players skate around the near circle then move to the adjacent circle skating in the opposite direction.
- Players proceed to the center circle and then to the far two circles.
- The next three players start when the previous group has completed the first circle.

Key Teaching Points
- Encourage players to keep knees bent on the corners.
- Emphasize high leg crossovers.
- Emphasize improving crossovers in both directions.
- Emphasize holding the stick with two hands while skating forward and using one hand while skating backwards.

EXPANSION

#1. Players bring their legs up very high on their crossovers to increase the difficulty.

#2. Five-Circle Look-One-Way Drill, where players must keep looking at the opposite end of rink while skating around all five circles. They must also make forward and backward transitions twice on each circle.

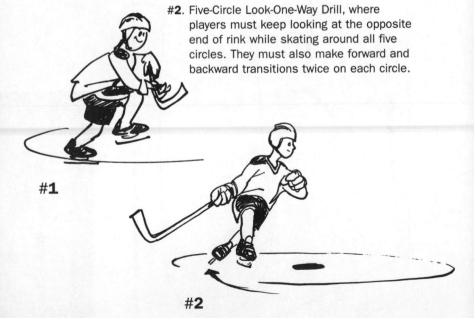

#1

#2

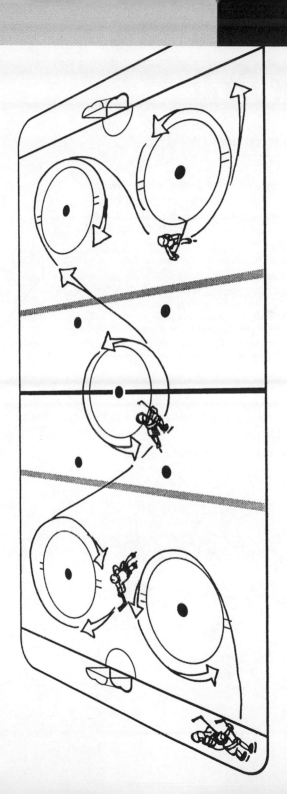

FIVE-CIRCLE SKATING

Shadow Drill

Objective
To develop quick turns and better agility

Description
- Divide the group into pairs with equal skating ability.
- One player is the skater; the other is his shadow.
- All players stay in mid-ice between the blue lines.
- On a whistle, the skater tries to lose his shadow while the shadow tries to stay close.
- Stop the drill with the whistle after five to seven seconds to ensure high-speed skating.
- Players then change roles and repeat.

Key Teaching Points
- Encourage players to keep their heads up while skating.
- Promote good footwork in tight spaces.
- Encourage quick reactions to directional changes.

EXPANSION

#1. Players stay in the space between the blue and red lines, then inside the center circle only.

#2. All players stickhandle pucks during the drill.

#2

SHADOW DRILL

Combination Circle and Diagonal Skating

Objective
To develop speed, agility and ice awareness

Description
- Divide the team into two groups starting in opposite corners of the rink.
- One group skates the five circles quickly, two players at a time.
- The other group skates diagonally, blue to red to blue line.
- Players keep their heads up while proceeding through the mid-ice area.
- Groups switch after completing a full rotation.

Key Teaching Points
- Encourage players to keep their knees bent using a strong push during crossovers.
- Encourage players to keep their heads up while skating through the mid-ice area.
- Encourage high-intensity skating.

EXPANSION

#1. Players skate backwards throughout the drill.

#2. Players stickhandle pucks while skating.

#1

#2

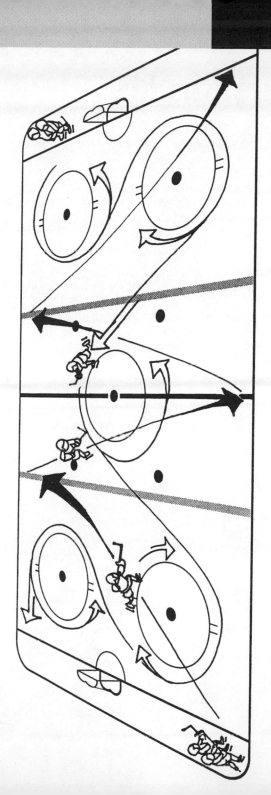

Skate the Circles

Objective
To develop forward and backward agility skating

Description
- Start players in two diagonal corners of the rink.
- The first player begins skating around the near circle, through pylons positioned in the mid-ice zone, and around the far circle.
- The second player starts after the previous skater completes the first circle.

Key Teaching Points
- Encourage players to keep their knees bent on crossovers with a low center of gravity.
- Encourage players to keep two hands on the stick while skating forward and one hand while going backward.
- Encourage high-speed skating between pylons.

EXPANSION

#1. Perform full 360° circles around each pylon.

#2. Players stickhandle pucks while skating through the course.

#1

#2

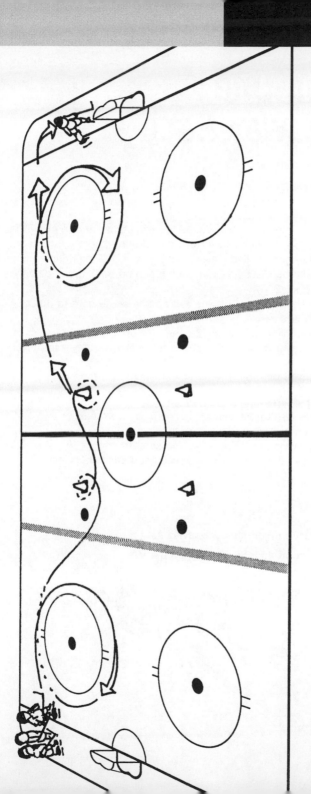

SKATE
THE CIRCLES

One-on-One Breakaway Race

Objective
To develop quick skating speed from a stop

Description
- Divide players into two equal groups in each corner at one end of the rink. If there is a discrepancy of size and skating talent on the team, then have the more skilled players perform the drill together.
- Begin play with the first player in each group on both knees directly on the goal line.
- On a whistle, the first two players get up and skate hard to a puck set in the mid-ice zone.
- The first player to reach the puck continues on a breakaway.
- The second player tries to stick check the offensive player to prevent a goal.
- Players return to the opposite line by skating down the boards.

Key Teaching Points
- Encourage players to practice proper recovery from being down on the ice.
- Encourage players to employ explosive acceleration.
- Encourage the trailing player to practice good stick checking technique.

EXPANSION

#**1**. Players start on their stomachs lying flat on the ice.

#**2**. Players start on their backs lying on the ice.

#1

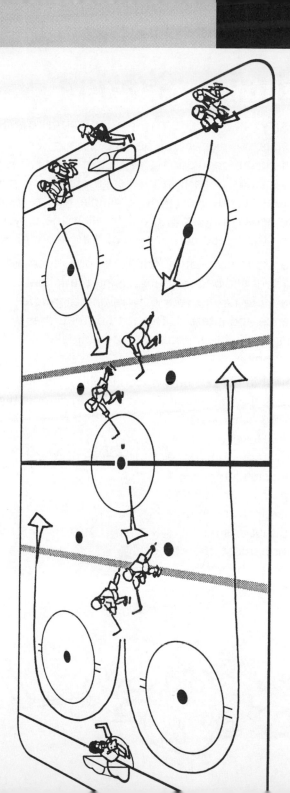

ONE-ON-ONE BREAKAWAY RACE

Conditioning Skating

A HIGH INTENSITY PRACTICE WITH FEW INTERRUPTIONS provides a valuable component of aerobic fitness for players. To supplement the conditioning aspect of a practice, it is worthwhile to include drills that challenge players to perform at high intensity. However, provide ample rest periods between intense activity bursts in order to allow the players to further develop the speed component of their skating.

Although there are many skating drill variations, such as line skating and over-and-back skating, using the following drills may be more fun for your players and therefore improve compliance and interest. Because of that, these drills may be more valuable in improving skating skills, speed and conditioning.

Possibly the most important part of conditioning skating for young players is the fun factor! Any coach can compel his players to complete exhausting conditioning drills. However, most players learn very early on to pace themselves in anticipation of further conditioning drills. An innovative coach will use interesting and challenging drills that ensure the players work their hardest, thereby helping to develop both skating, speed and conditioning.

Goalies should be expected to perform skating drills along with the team.

On the following pages are drills that focus on conditioning in order to produce an entire team of fit players. Goalies should be expected to perform these drills along with the team. These types of drills are recommended over the more traditional, monotonous drills that have been used in the past. An insightful coach will notice a significant decline in practice intensity if he has his players skate repetitively back and forth across the rink. However, a coach who understands an athlete's psyche can use that player's excitement, competitive spirit and positive attitude to make conditioning drills some of the most high tempo components of a practice.

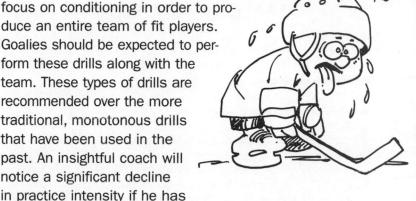

Innovators in hockey are not those who follow the standards of years past. They continually challenge players to be the best they can be by using creative drill selection and positive mentorship.

CONDITIONING
SKATING

Full-Lap Stick Relay

Objective
To improve conditioning and to encourage full-speed skating

Description
- Divide players into four equal teams.
- Move the goal nets in toward mid-ice slightly to give more room to skate behind the net.
- The first player on each team lines up on one side of the centerline.
- All other players slowly skate in a tight circle around the center circle of the rink.
- On a whistle, the first player on each team skates as fast as he can around both nets on the perimeter of the ice surface. He carries a stick for use as the "baton" to pass off to his teammates.
- As the first player comes around the final corner and approaches the centerline, a second teammate leaves the inner "track" and begins skating faster.
- The first player hands off the baton (stick) to his teammate while both are skating, and the second player then completes the skating course.
- Each team member keeps track of when it is his turn to skate a fast lap.
- The race continues for a period of four or five minutes or until each player has completed four to six fast laps around the ice. The drill can be repeated as required for older players.
- End the drill if the intensity of skating is adversely affected by fatigue.

Key Teaching Points
- Create a fun, competitive environment to ensure maximum speed.
- Simulate a hockey shift, where players skate hard for 20 to 30 seconds, then reduce the intensity of their skating.
- Practice the relay both clockwise and counterclockwise.

EXPANSION

#1. Players skate backwards throughout the relay.

#2. Teams race where one teammate pushes another around the ice, then gets pushed by the next teammate in order. This drill expansion incorporates a component of power development into this skating relay.

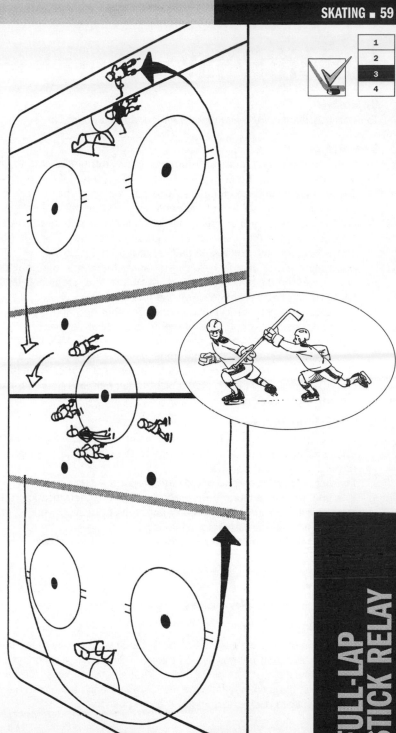

FULL-LAP
STICK RELAY

Parloff Relay

Objective
To enhance conditioning while developing speed and quick starts

Description
- Divide players into groups of three, and move in the goal nets to give more room behind the net.
- The first player in each group lines up on one side of the centerline, the second on the far end of the centerline, and the third directly behind the first player, all facing either clockwise or counterclockwise.
- On a whistle, the first player in each group skates as quickly as he can behind the net, continuing halfway around the ice.
- As the first player approaches his stationary teammate on the opposite end of the centerline, he quickly skates to him, stops and tags his partner, effectively handing off the role of skater.
- The second player skates hard around the other net, and the first player stays on the centerline where he tagged his partner.
- Once the second player has completed a half lap, he tags the third teammate and stays on the centerline while his partner speeds off.
- The race among all teams continues for a period of four or five minutes or until each player has completed eight to ten half laps (more for older players) around the ice.

Key Teaching Points
- Encourage players to keep their knees bent to improve leg extension.
- Encourage players to extend their legs to the side while skating, rather than straight backward.
- Instruct team members to coordinate proper tag sequence.
- It is important to ensure the players do not leave their location until they have been touched by a teammate, thus effectively working on quick starts from a stationary position.
- Perform the drill skating both clockwise and counterclockwise.

EXPANSION

#1. Players pass a hockey stick as a baton.

#2. Players skate backwards through the race course.

#3. In teams of four, two players line up at the start line. One teammate pushes the other halfway around the ice. After coming to a complete stop, the pushing player gets pushed by the teammate waiting at the far centerline. The relay continues around the ice where each team member gets an opportunity to push a teammate, then be pushed.

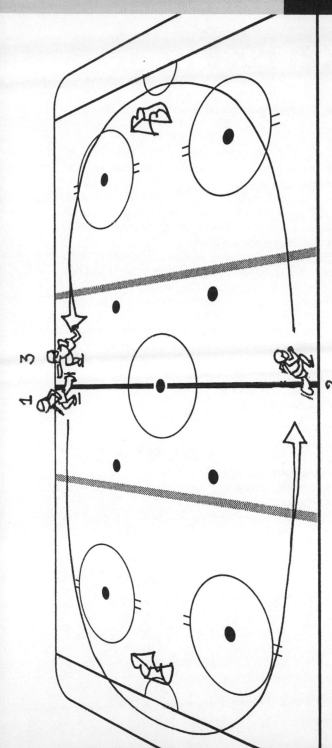

#1

#2

#3

PARLOFF RELAY

Stick-Steal Race

Objective

To improve conditioning and develop better skating awareness with a full speed competition

Description

- Divide players into four equal groups, each located in an end-zone circle.
- All players lay their sticks in the middle of their circle and line up at the top of the circle closest to center ice.
- On a whistle, the first player in each corner skates quickly in a diagonal direction across the ice to the opposite circle, ensuring that he keeps his head up through the mid-ice zone.
- On reaching the opposite circle, he picks up a stick, "steals it," then skates quickly back to his group, dropping the stick into the middle of their circle.
- Once a player enters his own circle, the next player in line can begin the race.
- Each group tries to "steal" more sticks than the other groups can. The championship group is the one that has the most sticks when the race is concluded.
- End the drill when the intensity of skating is adversely affected by fatigue or after an appropriate amount of conditioning.

Key Teaching Points

- Encourage friendly competition and high-intensity skating.
- Encourage players to practice picking up a hockey stick on the ice without removing a glove.
- The progression of shorter to longer skating distances is a good way of improving aerobic conditioning.

EXPANSION

Players skate backwards during the race.

STICK-STEAL
RACE

Full-Ice Horseshoe Skating

Objective

To improve conditioning and develop quick turns

Description

- Divide players into three groups, lined up in one corner of the rink.
- On a whistle, the first group skates full speed around the far net and back to the opposite side of the near blue line.
- After reaching the blue line, all players turn towards the boards and change directions without stopping and losing their skating momentum.
- The players return around the far net and skate back to the first corner.
- When all players in the group have completed the rotation, a whistle signals the next group to begin.
- Once all groups have completed their first rotation, repeat the drill to the opposite side of the centerline, the opposite far blue line, the far goal line, the same-side far blue line, same-side centerline, and finally the same-side near blue line.

Key Teaching Points

- Encourage full leg extension while striding.
- Instruct players to always turn towards the boards to prevent collisions and to practice turning both ways during the drill.
- The progression of shorter to longer skating distances is a good way of improving aerobic conditioning.

EXPANSION

Players skate the patterns backwards.

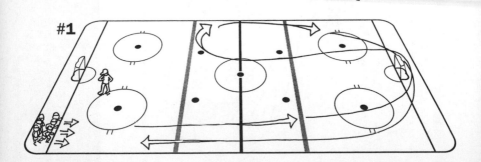

#1

#2

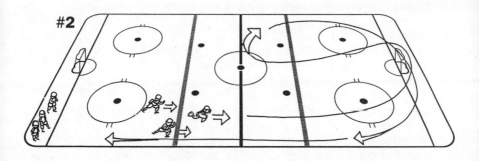

#3

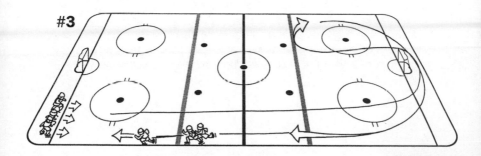

Line Skating

Objective
To improve player conditioning while developing better stops and starts

Description
- Divide players into two equal groups—the first lined up along one goal line and the other just behind the first.
- On a whistle, the first group skates quickly to the centerline, stops quickly, and skates back to the near blue line, then to the far blue line, then to the centerline, finally skating all the way to the opposite goal line.
- Once the first group has left the near blue line on their way to the far blue line, the second group can begin the drill.
- If the tempo of the drill decreases, then conclude the drill and move on to something new.

Key Teaching Points
- Encourage players to skate all the way to each line.
- Encourage players to always stop while looking towards one side of the rink to ensure they practice using both skate edges when stopping.
- This drill has been a standard for many coaches over the years, but it is only effective if the players perform the skating at a consistently high intensity.

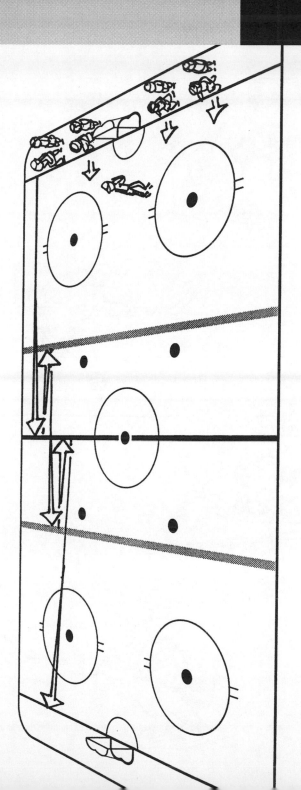

Agility Drills

Agility Drills

Definition—*the skill that allows a player to change directions quickly and under full control*

IN A FAST-PACED GAME LIKE HOCKEY, THE ABILITY TO change directions quickly and easily in response to a change in puck direction is a valuable skill. The greatest players, both offensively and defensively, use their agility, balance and coordination in every game to create goal-scoring opportunities and make spectacular game-saving plays.

Wayne Gretzky may be the best example of a player who used uncanny agility to his advantage. Not blessed with amazing speed or overpowering strength, Wayne dominated the game of hockey for years because of his unmatched ice awareness and skating agility. It was not unusual to see an opposing player lining him up for a check when in an instant, Wayne read the situation, made a quick direction change to avoid the check, and seemingly without effort, made a perfect tape to tape pass to an open teammate. I can remember only once or twice in Wayne's career that he was solidly hit

by an opposing player. That's an amazing statistic considering he is the National Hockey League's all-time leading scorer.

On the following pages are drills that focus on agility. Improving one's agility is a great way of increasing offensive performance and reducing the chance of injuries from heavy body checks. Goalies should be expected to perform agility drills along with the team where possible.

Goalies should be expected to perform skating drills along with the team.

AGILILTY DRILLS

Full-Rink Skating

Objective
To develop agility while working on recovery and balance

Description
- Divide players into two groups, lining up one group along one goal line and the other directly behind the first.
- On a whistle, the first group skates hard to the other end of the rink.
- As soon as the first group reaches the near blue line, the second group begins skating.

Key Teaching Points
- Encourage quick tempo.
- Encourage players to sprint at full speed for the first few strides from a stationary position.

OPTIONS
#1. As they proceed down the ice, players perform two-footed jumps over the near blue line, centerline and far blue line as they skate.

#2. Players go down on both knees at each line and hop back up, continuing on to the next line.

#3. Players balance on one leg from the centerline to the far end of the rink.

#4. Players perform a full squat at the centerline and hold it until all the way to end of the rink.

#5. Players perform an Alligator Roll at the centerline—go down on the stomach, do a complete roll and get back up.

#1

#2

#3

#4

#5

Backwards Crossover Drill

Objective
To improve backwards skating and balance

Description
- Line up all players close to one goal line facing the end boards and the coach.
- Players skate backwards with crossover strides.
- Use a stick to point to the direction of the crossover.
- Players should work on agility and quickness with quick direction changes.

Key Teaching Points
- Encourage players to keep knees bent, head up and one hand on the stick.
- Encourage players to keep shoulders square during crossovers.
- Encourage quick transitions to another direction.
- Skating speed is not important. The key is to work on lateral movement and proper crossover technique.

Stick-Direction Drill

Objective
To develop four-direction agility

Description
- Have players spread out around the center ice area.
- Be at one end with a stick in the air.
- Players follow the direction of the stick—forward, backward, lateral crossovers, down on knees.
- Promote quick direction changes.
- Work for a short time, 10 to 15 seconds, but at full speed.

Key Teaching Points
- Encourage players to perform quick skating transitions.
- Encourage players to keep their heads up while skating.
- Encourage players to sprint on the first few strides from a stationary position.
- Allow ample rest between drill segments to promote high-intensity skating.

EXPANSION
Players stickhandle pucks during the drill.

STICK-DIRECTION
DRILL

Crossover Line Skating

Objective
To develop speed and acceleration with lateral crossovers

Description
- Have players start in one corner of the rink.
- The first player skates fast to the near blue line.
- He stops at the blue line and performs full-ice crossovers across the complete length of the blue line.
- The player then skates up to the centerline, stops and crosses over the entire distance of the centerline.
- He then skates to the far blue line and crosses over in a similar manner.
- The next player begins when the previous one reaches the first blue line.

Key Teaching Points
- Encourage quick leg movement.
- Encourage players to keep hips and shoulders square when crossing over.
- Encourage players to keep eyes up and knees bent.

EXPANSION

Players cross a foot behind the other rather than in front. This is a challenge for most players at first, but they soon master the skill. It reinforces the importance of keeping the knees bent and the body balanced at all times.

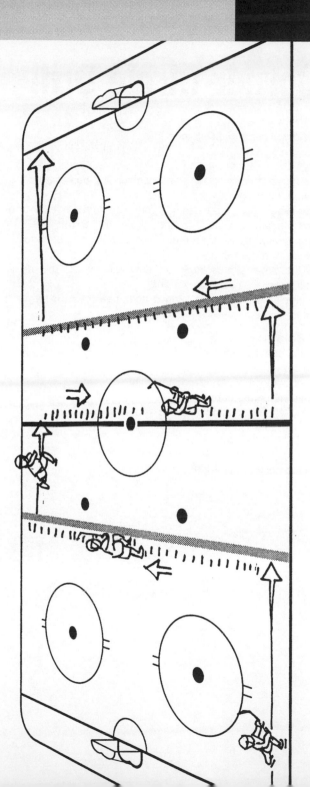

CROSSOVER
LINE SKATING

Four-Corner Circle Drill

Objective
To develop quick transitions in tight spaces

Description
- Divide players into five equal groups and position a group at each corner circle and the center circle.
- The first player skates from the bottom of the circle to the middle, and back to the bottom, always looking towards the middle of the ice.
- The player then skates up to the middle, over to one side, back to the middle, and up to the top.
- From the top, the player skates back to the middle, over to the other side, the middle and finally, to the bottom.
- Each player completes a full-circle skating drill, then the next player begins the drill.

Key Teaching Points
- Encourage quick direction changes.
- Encourage good foot speed.
- Promote proper balance when moving laterally.
- Emphasize quickness and bent knees.
- Watch for heads up and minimal hip and shoulder rotation.

EXPANSION
Players stickhandle pucks while skating.

Backwards Tightrope

Objective
To improve balance while performing a difficult outside edge skating drill

Description
- Divide the players into two equal groups, one lined up on the goal line and the other directly behind.
- Players in the first group skate backwards in a bent-knee defensive position.
- Have players lift their forward skates up and place them behind the rear skates.
- Players continue down the ice, repeating the movement.
- The second group begins skating when the first group has reached the near blue line.

Key Teaching Points
- Encourage good defensive skating positioning.
- Encourage players to keep knees bent, head up, and one hand on the stick.
- This maneuver simulates a reverse backward skating stride. It also works the outside edges skating backwards. It is difficult to do and much practice is needed for mastery.
- Emphasize technique, not speed.

1
2
3
4

BACKWARDS TIGHTROPE

Stick-Dive Drill

Objective
To develop agility and quick recovery after falling to the ice

Description
- Line up players on the goal line in the same number of lines as there are coaches.
- Coaches kneel at the centerline with a stick extended 2 feet above the ice surface.
- One by one, players skate fast and dive under the sticks.
- The next player begins skating after the previous player reaches the near blue line.

Key Teaching Points
- Encourage players to skate as fast as they can.
- Encourage players to dive as flat as possible.
- Encourage quick recovery, getting back up on two feet.
- Encourage quick recovery from the prone position back to full speed skating again.

EXPANSION
Lower the level of the stick to make the drill more challenging.

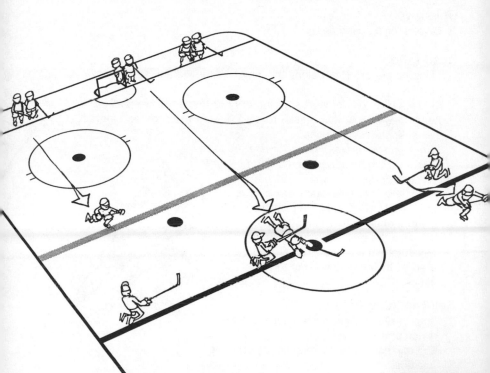

STICK-DIVE
DRILL

Figure-Eight Look-One-Way Race

Objective
To develop high speed agility

Description
- Line up players singly along the length of the ice and spread out evenly.
- Place two pylons or gloves 10 meters (30 feet) equally apart for each player. It is often easier to have players use their own gloves as substitutes for pylons.
- On a whistle, players skate forward around the far pylon, then backwards returning to the near pylon.
- When they reach the near pylon, players pivot forward again and repeat the course three or four times.
- Develop the drill into a fun race to encourage full speed.
- Repeat the entire drill up to three times.

Key Teaching Points
- Encourage players to keep knees bent when crossing over.
- Encourage players to keep heads up while skating.
- Encourage players to keep two hands on the stick while skating forward and one hand on the stick while skating backwards.

EXPANSION
Players stickhandle pucks while skating.

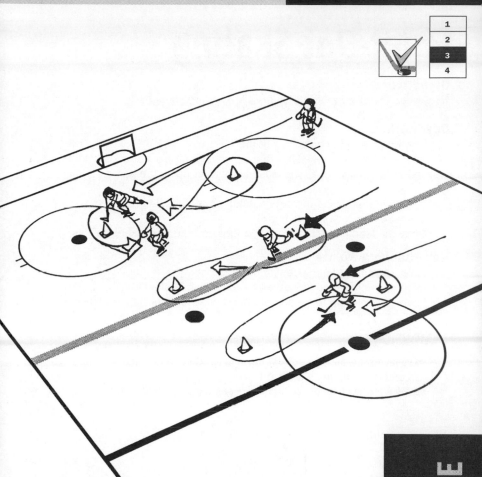

FIGURE-EIGHT
LOOK-ONE-WAY RACE

Eight-Dot Skating

Objective
To develop improved footwork and quick direction changes

Description
- Line up players in one corner of the rink.
- One at a time, players skate to the opposite corner dot and circle it.
- The skater proceeds to the close corner dot using the same circling maneuver.
- He continues around the dots outside both blue lines and in the opposite end zone.
- Once the lead player is around the first dot, the next skater begins.

Key Teaching Points
- Encourage quick foot speed around the dots.
- Encourage players to keep their heads up while skating.
- Encourage players to keep their knees bent to allow tighter corners.

EXPANSION

#1. Players do complete 540° turns around each dot. (540° is one and one-half times around the dot.)

#2. Players stickhandle pucks while skating around the dots.

#2

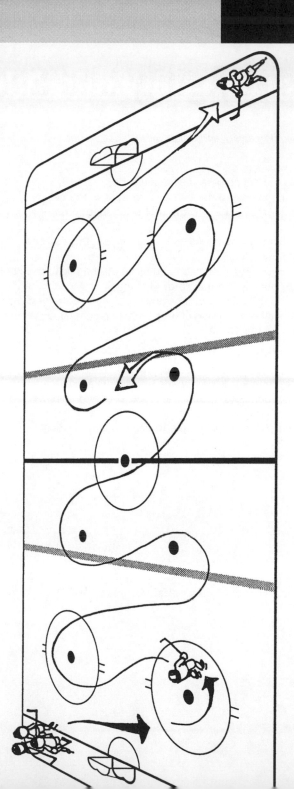

EIGHT-DOT SKATING

Defensive Agility and Shot

Objective
To develop good skating agility and finish with a shot on net

Description
- Station players in both corners of the end zone.
- Set a puck in the middle of the slot area in front of the net.
- The first player skates quickly to the first pylon then turns backwards.
- The player skates backward hard to the next pylon, then skates forward to the final pylon.
- He continues around the last pylon and picks up the puck for a shot.
- Set up the next puck in the middle of the slot.
- The first player in the other group begins the drill once the first player has completed half of the pylon course, ensuring continuous motion and challenges for the goalie.

Key Teaching Points
- Encourage quick foot speed around the pylons.
- Encourage players to keep their heads up while skating.
- Encourage good momentum to the net for a shot and possible rebound.
- Emphasize hard shots and attempts to score on any rebound.

Speed Drills

Speed Drills

Definition—*the ability to get from one position on the ice to another in the shortest time possible*

OVER THE LAST 20 YEARS, PROFESSIONAL HOCKEY HAS been transformed from a game of size, strength and power to a game where skating speed is likely the most important of the physical hockey skills. Young players can master the skills of passing, stickhandling and shooting through constant repetition; however, none of these skills will take a player to a higher level of ability like explosive skating speed.

During the height of Mark Messier's career, he was known as a tough, powerful forward with an amazing snap shot from his off wing. Not so well remembered were his amazing speed and quickness that enabled him to pounce on loose pucks. His teammates had the opportunity to see this quality every day at practice, and we came to understand that even a physically dominating player like Mark could develop high-speed skills through practice and hard work.

The influx of European players into the National Hockey League has strengthened the notion that skating speed is a valuable skill. Having developed their hockey skills on inter-national-sized ice surfaces, these players have the ability to consistently play at top speed.

On the following pages are drills that focus on skating speed. You can give your players the best chance to succeed in hockey by using at least one of these drills at every practice. Goalies should be  expected to perform speed drills along with the team when they are not needed in the net.

> *Goalies should be expected to perform speed drills along with the team when they are not needed in the net.*

Line-to-Line Sprint

Objective
To develop explosive skating starts

Description
- Divide the players into two equal groups, one group lined up on the goal line and the other directly behind.
- On a whistle, the first group takes three sprinting strides.
- They stop at the near blue line, always facing the same side of rink.
- With the next whistle, they begin skating again with three explosive strides to the far blue line.
- On the final whistle, players sprint to the far goal line.
- Once the first group has skated to the near blue line, the second group can also begin the drill at the sound of the whistle.
- Once both groups have finished skating to the opposite end, repeat back to other end, this time stopping while facing towards the same side of rink as before, thereby practicing stopping in both directions.

Key Teaching Points
- Encourage players to keep their knees bent for best skating thrust.
- Emphasize that the first three strides are the most important in developing quickness.
- Encourage players to practice stopping in both directions, facing towards one side of rink throughout the drill.
- Emphasize explosive first three strides.

EXPANSION

Players stickhandle pucks while sprinting.

| 1 |
| 2 |
| 3 |
| 4 |

LINE-TO-LINE
SPRINT

Line-Sprint Skating

Objective
To develop quick acceleration to full speed

Description
- Have players skate full-ice circles around the perimeter of the rink.
- They increase to full speed at the near blue line.
- They slow down to warmup pace at the far blue line.
- Players change direction on the whistle and repeat the drill.

Key Teaching Points
- Encourage strong leg thrust.
- Encourage players to keep knees bent when under their bodies.
- Emphasize working on speed-stride technique.
- Emphasize working from bent knees to full leg extension and toe push off.

EXPANSION

Players stickhandle pucks while skating.

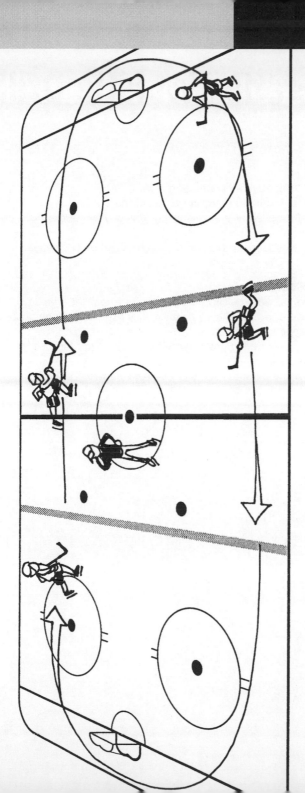

LINE-SPRINT SKATING

Acceleration Whistle Drill

Objective
To reach full speed at the sound of a whistle

Description
- Players skate full-ice circles in one direction.
- They listen for a whistle to start and to finish the sprint.
- Players skate full speed at the whistle; they slow down at the next whistle.
- After several repetitions, have players change direction and repeat the drill.

Key Teaching Points
- Instruct players to skate quickly as soon as they hear the whistle.
- Encourage players to have the striding leg fully extended during push-off with the support knee bent.
- Keep sprint time short, allowing players to go full speed for a short time and allowing ample rest time.
- Ensure that players perform the drill in both directions.

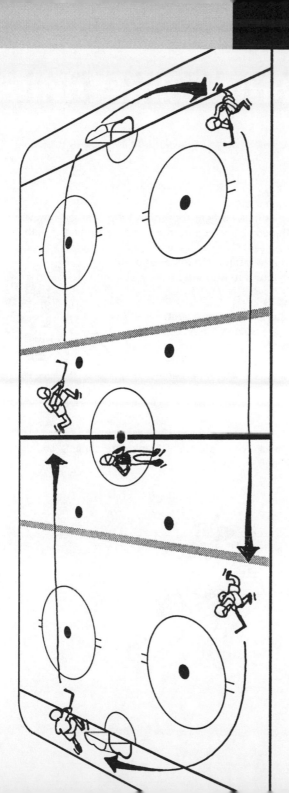

ACCELERATION
WHISTLE DRILL

Quick-Turn Whistle Drill

Objective
To react to the whistle and to perform quick turns followed by explosive strides

Description
- Players skate full-ice circles.
- On a whistle, players make a tight turn toward the boards—always turning towards the boards to ensure they practice turning in both directions.
- Players perform the first three strides after a turn at full speed then return to warmup pace.

Key Teaching Points
- Encourage quick turns with knees bent.
- Ensure the first three strides after a turn are explosive.
- Blow the whistle every 15 to 20 seconds.
- Emphasize bent knees through the tight turns.

EXPANSION

Players stickhandle pucks while sprinting. Emphasize cupping and controlling the puck through the turn.

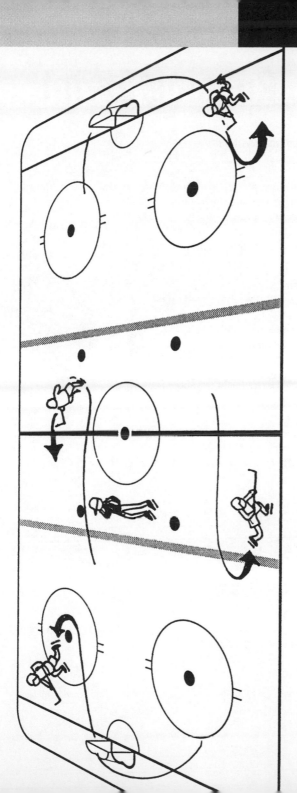

QUICK-TURN
WHISTLE DRILL

Full-Ice Running Sprint

Objective
To develop high-speed accelerations

Description
- Divide players into two groups, the first group lined up along one goal line and the other group directly behind.
- On a whistle, they try to run on their skates to the other end of the rink.
- Players must stay up on skate blades running, not skating.

Key Teaching Points
- Encourage players to stay up on toes, running rather than skating.
- Encourage players to proceed at full speed as far as possible.
- Encourage players to keep their knees bent for stronger thrust.
- Encourage players to keep knees bent for better balance.

EXPANSION
Players stickhandle pucks while running on their skates.

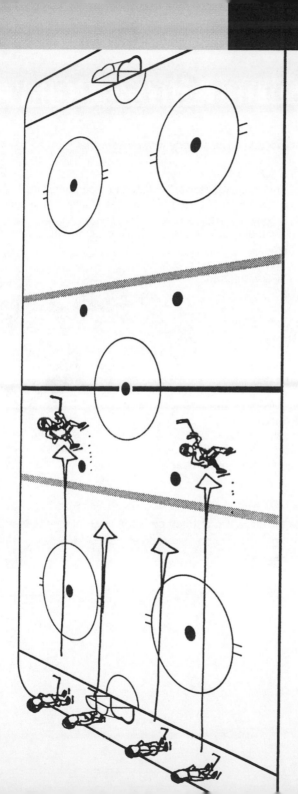

FULL-ICE
RUNNING SPRINT

Four-Corner Circle Relay

Objective
To encourage teamwork and quick skating with crossovers

Description
- Divide the team into four groups, each located in a corner circle.
- On a whistle, the first player in each group skates quickly to the center circle.
- Players skate around the circle in the same direction and then directly back to their group.
- The next player only leaves the circle when the first player returns to the home circle.

- Players go down on one knee when finished skating. The first team finished is the winner.
- Repeat the drill with all players skating in the opposite direction.

Key Teaching Points
- Encourage explosive skating.
- Encourage players to keep their heads up and knees bent.
- Promote having fun with a relay race.

EXPANSION

#1. Players skate the circle two or three times before returning to their groups.

#2. Bucket Relay, page 108.

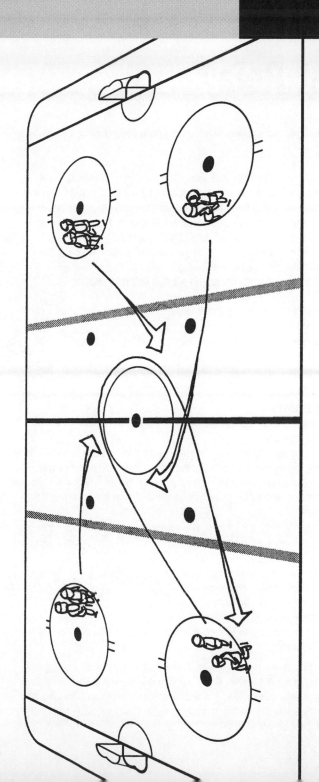

FOUR-CORNER
CIRCLE RELAY

Bucket Relay

Objective

To enhance proper knee bend when skating and promote good weight transfer

Description

- Players perform this drill like the Four-Corner Circle Relay, except that the first skater in each group holds onto a large bucket turned upside down. (These buckets are often available at arena concessions as they are frequently used to package bulk foods. Optimal size for these buckets is 60–75 cm [24–30 inches] high.)
- Players skate around the outside of the center circle keeping the inside hand on top of the bucket.
- Players keep knees well bent, staying in a more efficient skating position.
- Players extend inside arms towards the center of the circle to get more comfortable with angling the body while skating around a corner.
- Players practice to become more proficient at leaning inward when going around a corner. Performing this drill regularly produces more effective skaters.

Key Teaching Points

- Encourage skating with bent knees and with inside hand always holding the bucket.
- Instruct players to extend the inside arm holding the bucket to the inside and toward the center of the circle, rather than in front of the player.
- Encourage players to get used to leaning at an angle as they skate around the circle in order to enhance speed development and improved agility.

EXPANSION

One player sits on the bucket and tries to steer with his feet while a second player pushes from behind. Rotate the team through the drill with each player first pushing the bucket, then sitting on it while being pushed. The drill is finished when all players have pushed and been pushed on the bucket.

This drill is fun as players have a great deal of difficulty maneuvering the bucket around such a tight circle. It incorporates a power component to the drill for the players pushing and a leg strength component for the sitting players as their hamstring leg muscles are actively working to keep the bucket going in the correct direction.

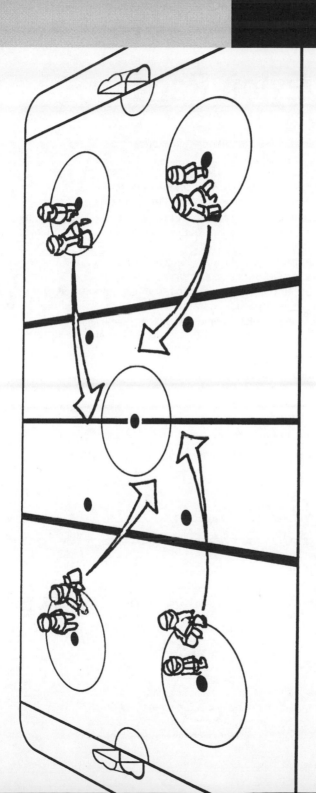

BUCKET RELAY

Pairs Pylon Race

Objective
To practice a one-on-one competition for the puck

Description
- Line two groups up in the corners of one end zone.
- Place two pylons just outside the blue line on the face-off dots.
- Each lead player starts the race by standing in the corner touching the red line on the end boards equally. This ensures that no player gets an unfair advantage.
- On a whistle, both lead players skate around the pylons to reach a loose puck located in the slot area.
- The first player to reach the puck tries to make a shot while the second player tries to check the shooter.
- When the play is complete, begin the next pair with a whistle.
- Set up the puck for each pair in the middle of the slot area.

Key Teaching Points
- Encourage quick acceleration around pylons.

EXPANSION

#1. Start players on their knees.

#2. Start players on their stomachs, lying flat on the ice.

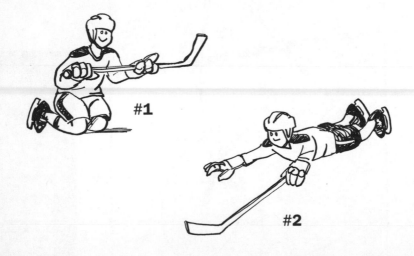

#1

#2

1
2
3
4

Team Full-Ice Relay

Objective
To encourage development of speed in a player's skating stride

Description
- Divide the team into two or three groups and position half of each group at opposite ends of the rink.
- Set up a pylon course down the ice for each group.
- On a whistle, the first player in each line begins skating through one end of the pylon course.
- Upon reaching the other end, each player tags a teammate who then skates back in the other direction. The group is finished when all members have completed the course three or four times.

Key Teaching Points
- Encourage explosive strides with knees bent.
- Encourage low center of gravity around pylons.
- Encourage team spirit in competition.

EXPANSION

#1–#3. Have players do full 360° pylon turns, skate backwards, stickhandle pucks.

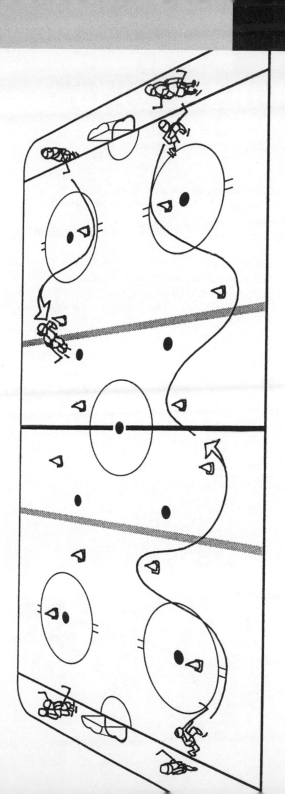

Tight-Turn Breakaways

Objective
To develop quick turns and high-speed accelerations

Description
- Start two groups in both corners of one end zone.
- On a whistle, the first two players skate around pylons placed in a slalom course in the defensive end of the rink.
- Once through the pylons, they race towards a puck that is placed in the center zone.
- The first player to reach the puck continues on a breakaway.
- The second player tries to check the first player to prevent a goal.
- Both players return to their own end by skating down the boards.
- The next pair begins when the preceding two players have reached the far blue line.

Key Teaching Points
- Encourage players to keep knees bent around the turns.
- Encourage high-energy acceleration coming out of the turns.
- Encourage players to try to stick check if they are behind on a breakaway.

EXPANSION

#1. Start players on both knees.

#2. Start players on their stomachs, lying flat on the ice.

#1

#2

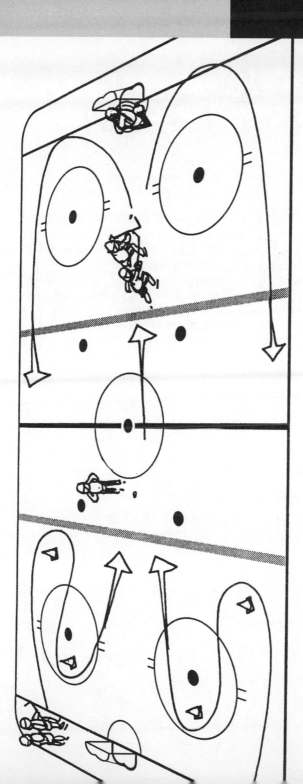

One-on-One Curl and Breakaway

Objective
To develop skating speed and ability to accelerate laterally

Description
- Start players in two lines at mid-ice.
- Place a puck in the middle of the offensive blue line.
- On a whistle, the first players in each line skate around pylons located on the centerline close to the mid-ice boards.
- Both players return to the middle of the ice to begin a breakaway.
- The first player to reach the puck continues on a breakaway.
- The second player tries to check the puck carrier to prevent a goal.
- Both return to the lineup by skating down the boards.
- The next pair begins when the preceding two players have reached the goal and have taken a shot.

Key Teaching Points
- Encourage quick turns around pylons.
- Encourage players to keep knees bent during turns.
- Encourage players to maintain good body position to protect the puck.

EXPANSION

#1. Start players on both knees.

#2. Start players on their stomachs, lying flat on the ice.

#1

#2

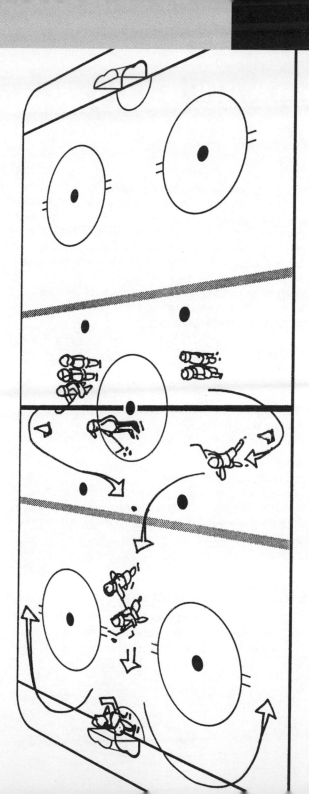

ONE-ON-ONE CURL
AND BREAKAWAY

Half-Lap Stick Relay

Objective
To improve full-speed skating and teamwork

Description
- Divide the team into groups of four or five players.
- The first player in each group lines up on one side of the centerline with a stick. All other players discard their sticks in a corner out of the way.
- The other players begin the relay on the inside track of the ice.
- On a whistle, the first players in each group race around the far net while all other players slowly circle in the same direction on the inside track.
- After skating halfway around the ice, the first player of each team "hands off" his stick to a teammate who has started speeding up and merged into the outside track.
- Once the handoff is made, the second player skates hard halfway around the ice while the first player rests, skating slowly around the inside track.
- Continue the race until all players have sprinted halfway around the ice at least five or six times or until it is apparent that the skating intensity has begun to drop off.

Key Teaching Points
- Encourage full-speed skating intervals.
- Encourage teamwork with coordinating stick handoffs.
- This drill is meant to be performed at top speed, since it simulates a hockey shift where players go hard for short periods of time then skate at more controlled speeds.

EXPANSION

#1. Players skate backwards.

#2. Pairs of players race. One teammate pushes another around the ice, then is pushed by the next teammate, thus incorporating a power development.

#1

#2

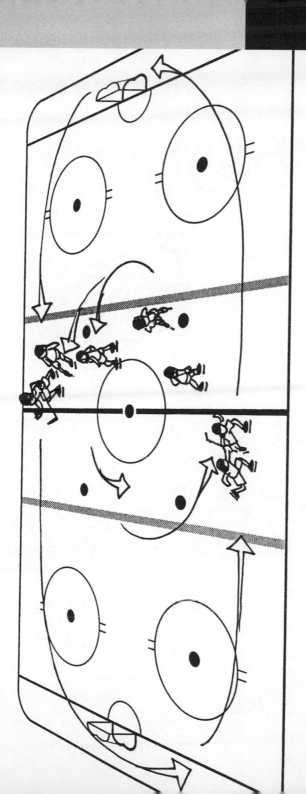

HALF-LAP
STICK RELAY

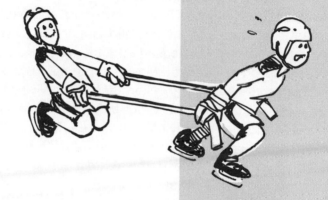

Power Drills

Power Drills

Definition—*the ability to skate effectively with a combination of speed and strength*

COLOR COMMENTATORS ON TELEVISION OFTEN COMMENT on how important it is for a hockey team to have a power forward who can control the corners offensively and easily fend off checking as he skates hard to the net. A championship team invariably has forwards like this who become important contributors to the overall team. In the past, training programs have often focused on either one of these attributes, speed or strength. Players often had explosive speed but could be easily knocked off the puck, whereas others were as strong as bulls, but unfortunately could never get to the play quickly enough to be effective. It is now known that one need not sacrifice speed to gain strength or vice versa. Indeed, these are two of the most important qualities that combine to make a complete hockey player.

While there are many dry-land drills that can effectively improve skating power, on-ice drills may also be used to develop power. On the following pages are drills that focus on power skills. It is important that players be informed of

Goalies should be expected to perform power drills along with the team.

the importance of performing these drills at high intensity, because they tend to be harder on the leg muscles and poorly conditioned players will fatigue quickly. Fortunately, many of the drills described are fun to do, so players will be more motivated to maintain high intensity. Goalies should be expected to perform power drills along with the team.

Stick-Jump Drill

Objective
To develop explosive leg extension and balance with knees bent

Description
- Divide the team into the same number of lines as coaches.
- Line up each group of players on one goal line.
- Coaches kneel at the centerline evenly spaced with a stick extended 30 centimeters (1 foot) above the ice.
- One by one players skate fast and jump over the sticks.
- Each player begins skating after the previous player reaches the near blue line.

Key Teaching Points
- Encourage players to keep their knees bent on take-off and landing.
- Instruct players not to rotate their hips using a one-footed take-off, but to use a two-footed jump instead.
- Encourage proper knee bending when landing.
- Encourage players' attempts at jumping over increasing stick heights, not just making successful jumps.

EXPANSION
Slowly progress to higher stick levels.

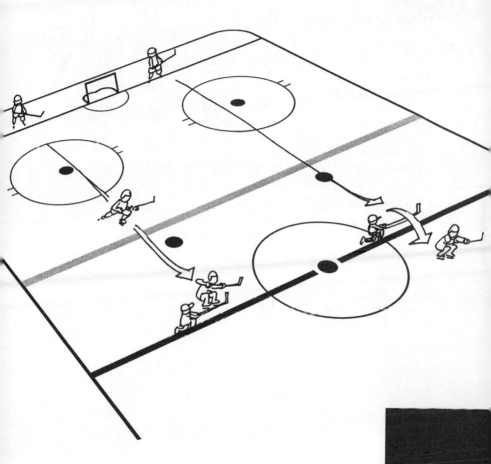

Partner Push Drill

Objective
To develop a powerful stride

Description
- Pair up players with equal or similar skating ability.
- Line them up at the goal line—both facing forward, one behind the other. Sticks are not needed.
- The rear skater pushes his partner down the ice.
- Skaters switch positions at the end of the rink, repeat the maneuver, and return to where they started.

Key Teaching Points
- Encourage players to keep knees bent; maintain good balance.
- Encourage partners to give moderate resistance to skating.

EXPANSION
The front player increases skating resistance by angling his skates in snowplow fashion, thereby making it more difficult for the rear player to push him down the ice.

1
2
3
4

**PARTNER
PUSH DRILL**

Partner Pull Drill

Objective
To develop a powerful stride

Description
- Pair up players with equal or similar skating ability.
- Line them up at one goal line, both players facing forward one behind the other.
- The lead skater holds both stick blades.
- The rear skater holds both stick knobs.
- On a whistle, the lead skater pulls his partner down the ice.
- The rear player resists moderately by partially digging his skate edges into the ice.
- Skaters switch positions at the end of the rink, repeat the maneuver, and return to where they started.

Key Teaching Points
- Encourage players to keep knees bent.
- Encourage players to use strong leg thrusts.
- Encourage moderate resistance from partners.

EXPANSION
Player pulls his partner while the partner is on his knees, then while he is lying down.

1
2
3
4

PARTNER
PULL DRILL

Pylon Quick-Turn Drill

Objective
To develop explosive power coming out of a turn

Description
- Arrange pylons around the outer edges of the rink.
- Divide players into two groups in opposite corners of the rink.
- On a whistle, the first player skates completely around the first pylon.
- He makes a quick turn and skates to the next pylon, going around it in the opposite direction.
- The next skater begins when the previous skater is through the first pylon.
- Players continue pylon skating all the way down the ice, and when finished, they line up in the opposite corner.

Key Teaching Points
- Encourage quick turns with a low center of gravity.
- Encourage explosive first three strides coming out of the turns.
- Emphasize the importance of a low center of gravity to improve turning efficiency.

EXPANSION
Players stickhandle pucks while skating.

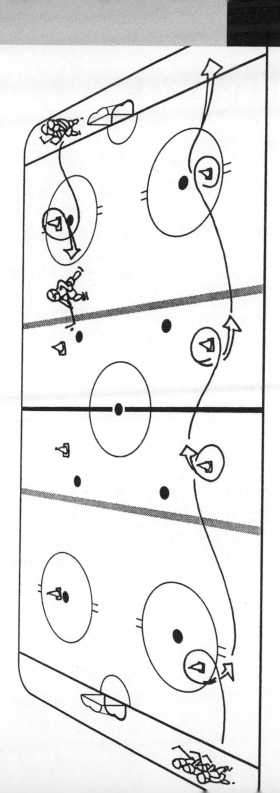

PYLON QUICK-
TURN DRILL

Stick Chain Race

Objective
To work as a team using powerful strides

Description
- Divide the team into four groups at one end of the ice.
- Players line up one behind the other and stay together by holding sticks.
- On a whistle, the groups race down to the pylons at the far face-off dots, circle them, and return to the start.
- Repeat the drill with the players in a different order.

Key Teaching Points
- Encourage coordinated skating.
- Promote teamwork.
- Teams must stay together. If they fall apart, then the team must stop and set up again.
- Emphasize teamwork.

EXPANSION

Only the lead player skates, while the others glide. The race is finished when all players have pulled their teammates down the ice and back.

STICK CHAIN
RACE

One-Knee Rotations

Objective
To develop powerful legs for improved skating

Description
- Divide the team into two equal groups with one group spread out across the goal line and the second group directly behind the first.
- On a whistle, the first group begins skating but with knees bent.
- They bend the right knee to touch the ice on the first stride.
- They touch the left knee to the ice on the next stride.
- Players continue alternating touching knees to the ice surface all the way down the rink.
- They stop at the opposite end of the rink.
- The second group begins skating when all of the players in the first group have reached the near blue line.

Key Teaching Points
- Encourage players to bend their knees as they skate all the way down the ice.
- Encourage players to increase the speed of knee movement as they become stronger.
- For younger players, run the drill only between the blue lines to minimize the potential for an overuse injury.

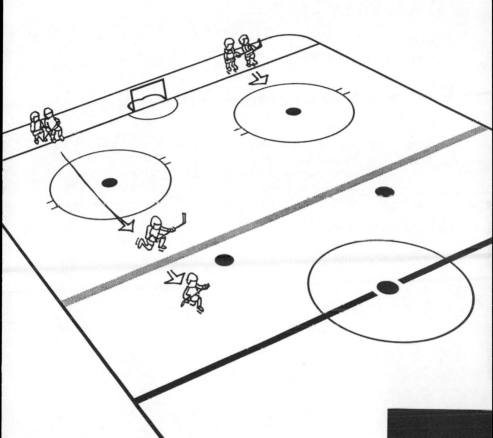

ONE-KNEE
ROTATIONS

Lateral Skating Accelerations

Objective
To develop high-speed lateral movement

Description
- Have players skate around the perimeter of the rink.
- At the blue lines, they accelerate quickly from the boards towards the inner part of the rink.
- At the centerline, they accelerate quickly from the inner part of the rink back out towards the boards.
- They slow down for a rest when skating around both nets.
- Players skate in one direction for three or four laps then switch to the opposite direction.

Key Teaching Points
- Encourage players to skate with high intensity using crossovers.
- Encourage players to accelerate from blue line to blue line.
- Encourage players to keep knees bent for a stronger thrust.

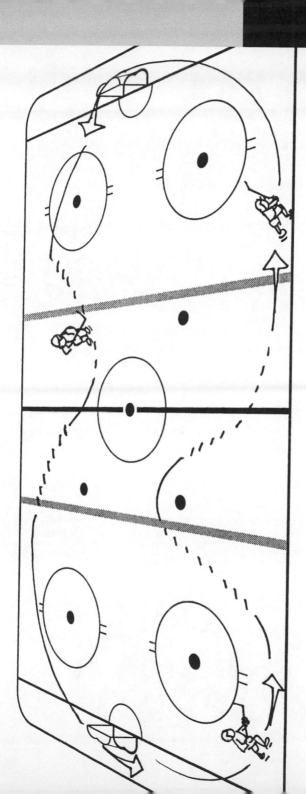

LATERAL SKATING
ACCELERATIONS

Caboose Race

Objective
To develop powerful legs for improved skating

Description
- Divide the team into groups of four players each. Sticks are not needed.
- Line players up in a train configuration with each player holding the person in front by the hips.
- Line all groups up on one side of the centerline.
- On a whistle, the last skater pushes his teammates around the rink once.
- The fourth teammate skates hard while the rest glide with knees bent.
- When they get back to the start, the skater then moves to the front of the train, and the new back skater begins to push.
- The drill is complete when all group members have been the "pusher."

Key Teaching Points
- Encourage teamwork.
- Encourage players to keep knees bent and thrust legs out with each stride.
- Coordinate team rotations.

EXPANSION
Players must stay connected to their groups but can make sideways arm contact with other teams. Ensure that players only push opposing players and do not punch.

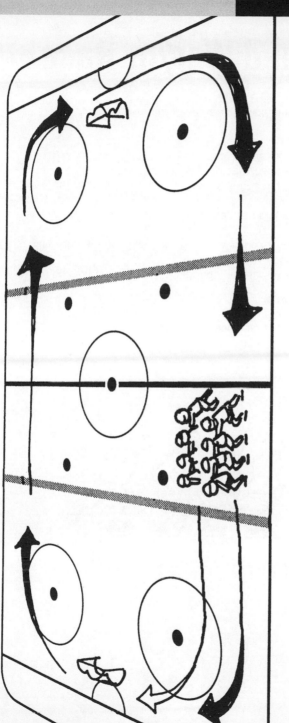

CABOOSE RACE

Horse and Wagon Race

Objective
To develop a strong and powerful stride for improved skating

Description
- Divide the team into groups of four.
- Groups line up in wagon-train fashion at the centerline.
- The first player is the horse, the other three are wagons. The wagons connect to the horse with their sticks.
- On a whistle, the horse skates around the rink for one lap, pulling the wagons.
- When the first horse completes a lap, he moves to the back and becomes a wagon.
- The drill is complete when all four players have been horses.

Key Teaching Points
- Encourage teamwork.
- Encourage skating at full speed for one lap.
- Make sure the players perform the drill in both directions.

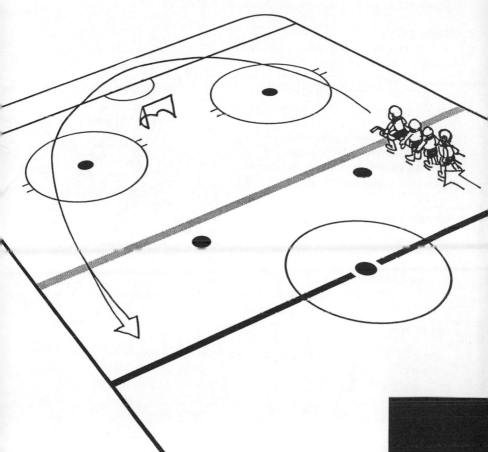

HORSE AND WAGON RACE

Mule Race

Objective
To develop powerful legs through increased skating resistance

Description
- Pair players up with those of equal size.
- Line up pairs at one end of the rink.
- One player hoists himself onto the back of his partner, the mule, holding on around the neck.
- On a whistle, the mule skates as fast as possible to the near blue line.
- The players exchange positions and continue to the far blue line.
- They exchange positions once more, and the mule skates to the far end of the rink.

Key Teaching Points
- Encourage working as partners.
- Promote proper carrying position before skating.
- This drill should only be performed by players who are experienced skaters in order to reduce the chance of injury.

EXPANSION
The mule carries his partner for a longer distance, up to the full length of the rink.

MULE RACE

Backwards Skating Tug of War

Objective
To develop powerful strides when skating backwards

Description
- Pair players up with those of equal size.
- Line pairs up facing each other at the centerline.
- One player holds two sticks, one in each hand. His opponent holds the opposite ends of the sticks.
- On a whistle, each player tries to pull his opponent backwards across his respective blue line.
- The challenge is complete when one player pulls the other fully across the blue line.
- Stop the drill when the intensity of the drill begins to decrease.

Key Teaching Points
- Encourage players to keep knees bent.
- Encourage full lateral pushoff with each backward stride.
- Stop the drill if players simply stand stationary and are not backward striding with full intensity.

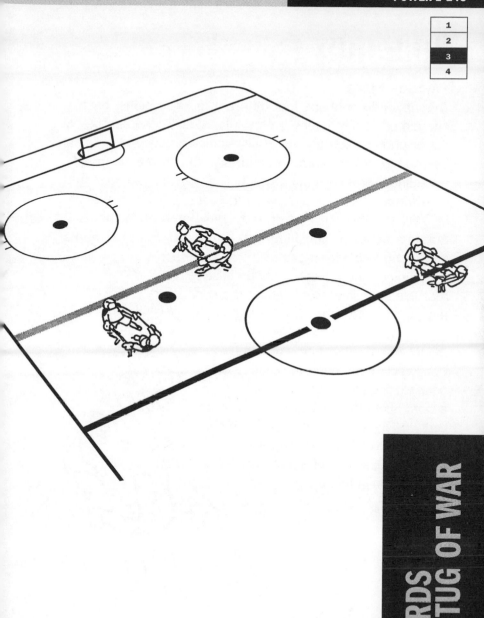

**BACKWARDS
SKATING TUG OF WAR**

Appendix

Practice Plans

This appendix contains four different practice plans, each one aimed at developing a particular skill. These can be cut out or photocopied and used as a quick practice plan or can be adapted to your own personal style. Each practice plan is outlined for a 60-minute practice and includes suggested time frames for each drill. Each includes a warmup, a skating drill and then several drills to develop a particular skill. Practice sessions conclude with a time for closing remarks and a short cooldown skate.

It is important to finish every practice with a couple of positive words about the good things that were done on the ice. It is a great way to have the players leave the ice in a positive frame of mind. Conversely, if the effort at practice was poor, closing off the session with a word about the things that the players could do better at the next practice still leaves them with a positive reference and good direction for a more productive session in the future.

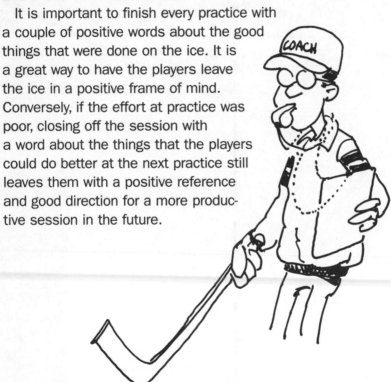

The cooldown laps are a good way of showing young players that, from a physiological standpoint, slowly cooling off with stretches and half-speed striding is a good way of allowing their muscles to recover after a hard workout.

Blank practice plans are reproducible and can be used to develop your own personal practice plans.

W

– Hockey Practice Plan 1 –
OBJECTIVE: Skating

Drill Name	From	To	Key Points
1. Double-Circle Warmup[1]	0	5	stretch/agility/warmup
2. Skating Fundamentals[1]	5	15	skating technique
3. Full-Lap Stick Relay[1]	15	20	speed/fun
4. Backwards Skating Tug of War[1] –Side Shuffle Technique[4]	20	25	power/balance
5. Defense-to-Wing Pass & Shoot[2]	25	35	positioning/team
6. Full-Ice Horseshoe[1]	35	50	1-on-0, 2-on-0, 3-on-0
7. Prisoner's Base[4]	50	58	agility/fun
8. Closing/Two Cooldown Laps	58	68	feedback/cooldown

minutes

Notes:

[1] Book 1: *Skating Drills for Hockey*
[2] Book 2: *Puck Control Drills for Hockey*
[3] Book 3: *Team Drills for Hockey*
[4] Book 4: *Advanced Drills & Goalie Drills for Hockey*

– Hockey Practice Plan 2 –
OBJECTIVE: Stickhandling

Drill Name	From	To	Key Points
1. Double-Circle Warmup[1]	0	5	stretch/agility/ warmup
2. Full-Rink Skating[1]	5	15	line jump/one knee/squat one leg balance/ alligator roll
3. British Bulldog[4]	15	20	agility/fun
4. Coach-Pylon-Rink Skating[2] –T-Push Technique[4]	20	25	agility/stickhandling
5. Figure-8 Glove Drill[2] –Letter Drill[4]	25	30	stickhandling
6. Jurassic Park[2] –Skipping Drill[4]	30	40	stickhandling
7. Pig in the Middle[2] –Behind-the-Net Control Drill[4]	40	50	passing/receiving
8. Train Race[4]	50	58	agility/fun
9. Closing/Two Cooldown Laps	58	60	feedback/cooldown

(minutes)

Notes:

[1] Book 1: *Skating Drills for Hockey*
[2] Book 2: *Puck Control Drills for Hockey*
[3] Book 3: *Team Drills for Hockey*
[4] Book 4: *Advanced Drills & Goalie Drills for Hockey*

– Hockey Practice Plan 3 –
OBJECTIVE: Team Play

Drill Name	From	To	Key Points
1. Double-Circle Warmup[1]	0	5	stretch/agility/ warmup
2. Full-Rink Skating[1]	5	10	line jump/one knee/squat one leg balance/ alligator roll
3. Parloff Relay[1]	10	15	agility/skating
4. Defensive Zone Positioning[3] –Down & Up Technique[4]	15	25	defensive zone awareness
5. Defensive Corner Breakout with 1-on-1[3]	25	35	easy breakout system
6. 5-on-0 Breakout Drill[3]	35	45	full team breakout options
7. Pig in the Middle[2] –T Drill[4]	45	50	passing, quick reaction
8. 3-on-3 Half-Ice Mini Hockey[4]	50	58	shooting
9. Closing/Two Cooldown Laps	58	60	feedback/cooldown

minutes (From / To)

Notes:

[1] Book 1: *Skating Drills for Hockey*
[2] Book 2: *Puck Control Drills for Hockey*
[3] Book 3: *Team Drills for Hockey*
[4] Book 4: *Advanced Drills & Goalie Drills for Hockey*

– Hockey Practice Plan 4 –
OBJECTIVE: Skating and Checking

Drill Name	From	To	Key Points
1. Double-Circle Warmup[1]	0	5	stretch/agility/warmup
2. Full-Lap Stick Relay[1]	5	10	speed/coordination
3. Stick-Jump Drill[1]	10	15	agility/fun
4. Bucket Relay[1]	15	22	skating speed
5. Defense-to-Wing-to-Center Pass & Shoot[2]	22	30	positioning/team play
6. 5-on-0 Breakout Drill[3]	30	40	team play
7. Around-the-Net Angle Drill[3]	40	45	checking technique
8. Direct Pinning Drill[3] –Mirror Drill[4]	45	50	checking technique
9. Full-Ice 1-on-1 Drill[3]	50	55	checking technique
10. Prisoner's Base[4]	55	58	agility/fun
11. Closing/Two Cooldown Laps	58	60	feedback/cooldown

Notes:

[1] Book 1: *Skating Drills for Hockey*
[2] Book 2: *Puck Control Drills for Hockey*
[3] Book 3: *Team Drills for Hockey*
[4] Book 4: *Advanced Drills & Goalie Drills for Hockey*

Hockey Practice Plan _____

OBJECTIVE: _____

Drill Name	From	To	Key Points
1.			
2.			
G—			
3.			
G—			
4.			
G—			
5.			
G—			
6.			
7.			
8.			
9.			

Hockey Practice Plan _____

OBJECTIVE: _____

Drill Name	From	To	Key Points
1.			
2.			
G—			
3.			
G—			
4.			
G—			
5.			
G—			
6.			
7.			
8.			
9.			

Hockey Practice Plan _____

OBJECTIVE: _____

	Drill Name	From	To	Key Points
1.				
2.				
G—				
3.				
G—				
4.				
G—				
5.				
G—				
6.				
7.				
8.				
9.				

Hockey Practice Plan _____

OBJECTIVE: _____

Drill Name	From	To	Key Points
1.			
2.			
G—			
3.			
G—			
4.			
G—			
5.			
G—			
6.			
7.			
8.			
9.			

Drill Index

C

D

E

F

H

I

L

M

Acknowlegments

A special thanks goes to the members of the Titans from Sherwood Park, Alberta, their friends, friends of Randy Gregg and parent volunteer Elliot Chiles for helping with the photo shoot for the covers of these books.

Top Row (L to R): Matthew Willard, Randy Gregg, Jared Phillips, Trevor Brophy
Middle Row (L to R): Jared Semen, Jade Chiles, Michael Budjak
Bottom Row (L to R): Jeremy Rockley, Cassidy Monaghan, Donald Anderson, Brandon Chunick , Chase Elliott, Alec Chomik
Goalie: Travis Bambush

We couldn't have done it without you!

OverTime Books

If you enjoyed *Skating Drills for Hockey,* be sure to check out these other great titles from OverTime Books:

PUCK CONTROL DRILLS FOR HOCKEY
by Randy Gregg

This is the second book in a series of four books for developing hockey skills for youth. Puck Control Drills for Hockey focuses on puckhandling, passing and shooting. This illustrated book provides a wide variety of easy-to-learn drills covering techniques for handling the puck in order to make scoring plays.

Softcover · 5.25" X 8.25" · $9.95 · 160 pages
ISBN10 0-9737681-6-9 · ISBN13 978-0-9737681-6-9

TEAM DRILLS FOR HOCKEY
by Randy Gregg

Book three in this four-book series provides easy-to-learn drills focusing on increasing the players' checking ability for all ages, as well as defensive and offensive zone play. The techniques in these drills help players create scoring opportunities for themselves and their team members.

Softcover · 5.25" X 8.25" · $9.95 · 144 pages
ISBN10 0-9737681-7-7 · ISBN13 978-0-9737681-7-6

ADVANCED DRILLS & GOALIE DRILLS FOR HOCKEY
by Randy Gregg

Book four of this four-book series contains team drills for teaching power plays and penalty killing for using odd-man situations to your team's advantage, transition plays from offensive to defensive strategy, goalie drills and games for putting the skills learned into play.

Softcover · 5.25" X 8.25" · $9.95 · 144 pages
ISBN10 0-9737681-8-5 · ISBN13 978-0-9737681-8-3

Each book contains:
· technical and dynamic drills for each skill,
· clear instructions for teaching and execution,
· descriptive diagrams for on-ice play,
· drill expansions for more advanced players,
· suggestions for getting the most out of a practice, and
· sample practice plans to help with organizing a complete practice.

Lone Pine Publishing is the exclusive distributor for OverTime Books. If you cannot find these titles at your local bookstore, contact us:

Canada 1-800-661-9017   **USA** 1-800-518-3541